FINAL

COMMITMENT

FINAL
COMMITMENT

An Anthology of MURDER in Old Berkshire

ROGER LONG

ALAN SUTTON PUBLISHING

BERKSHIRE BOOKS

First published by Berkshire Books in the United Kingdom in 1994 in association
with Alan Sutton Publishing Ltd · Phoenix Mill · Far Thrupp · Stroud
Gloucestershire

First published in the United States of America in 1994 by
Alan Sutton Publishing Inc. · 83 Washington Street · Dover · NH 03820

British Library Cataloguing in Publication Data
A catalogue record for this book is available from the British Library

ISBN 0-7509-0495-X

Library of Congress Cataloging in Publication Data applied for

Typeset in 10/13 Times.
Typesetting and origination by
Alan Sutton Publishing Limited.
Printed in Great Britain by
Redwood Books, Trowbridge,

CONTENTS

PREFACE

In 1990 I brought out my first book, *Murder in Old Berkshire*. It was an account of sixteen murders in the county. Most of these stories had never been published before.

In 1991 I followed this up with *I'll Be Hanged*, a further collection of some nineteen murders, and also an account of every unfortunate that had been hanged in the county for various other crimes. Again, most of these stories had never been published before.

Both books have been copied and plagiarized since on several occasions. I find this at the same time infuriating and slightly satisfying. To coin a phrase, imitation is still the sincerest form of flattery.

This foreword is by way of a protest. If one takes an anthology of crime from the shelf of any bookshop, one will find a rehashed, revamped collection of murder stories that have been displayed before the public for years. Ghost stories suffer much the same fate. It is the easiest thing in the world to select a couple of stories from several anthologies and serve them up lukewarm under differently categorized headings such as 'Coastal Murders', 'Theatre Murders', 'The Poisoners', 'The Lady Killers', 'The Unsolved', etc.; one could go on for ever.

There could hardly be a person of note in Victorian London who wasn't accused on tenuous grounds of being Jack the Ripper. Burke and Hare resurface with boring repetition. The Green Bicycle has left tyremarks over quite thirty anthologies. Poor Charlie can't rest in peace, he is resurrected regularly. We have been forcibly overdosed on Drs Palmer, Cream and Crippen, to mention nothing of Ruxton. We have been plagued by Christie, Hume and Haigh, and surely Thomas Allaway has more than had his day. We have been overgrazed on the brothers Kray. Ruth Ellis and Constance Kent keep us discontented. We have been misdirected by Thompson and saturated by Bywaters on a deluge of occasions. We have been gutted by poor PC Gutteridge and dished up with the cannibal Albert Fish until we have only the bones to stew, and so on and so on . . .

Add to the list above some hundred or so co-stars, who are nearly as well known, and one has encompassed probably 98 per cent of the true life murders published over the last fifty years.

It is not good enough. If more authors were to get off their backsides and research instead of plagiarizing each other into oblivion, they would discover a virtually untapped source of cornucopian proportions.

Final Commitment is a collection of eighteen further accounts of true felonious slayings in old Berkshire. At least twelve of these stories have never seen the light of day. One was completely stifled by a bureaucratic cover-up of massive proportions. Of the others, three have been extremely sparsely reported and the remaining two have been aired a little more extensively; these are the exceptions that prove the rule. Anyway I hope you enjoy them all.

ROGER LONG

CHAPTER ONE

1825 ETON: THE SLAYING OF THE HON. ASHLEY COOPER

On a freezing cold day in November 1912 the hallowed halls of Eton reverberated to the cry of 'Murder, murder' as the youthful scholars fled into the streets announcing the tragic slaying of Anne (Nancy) Davis by her rejected lover Eric Sedgewick.

Sedgewick met his maker at Reading on 4 February 1913 but the scandal attached to one of England's foremost schools was to remain for some considerable time. The stigma was to endure within the walls of respectability. Such incidents are eroded by the kindness of time not blotted out abruptly by the stroke of a pen or a hapless lover climbing the scaffold.

Eton, this bastion of all that is archetypal in the English aristocracy, had suffered the slings of discredit previously. Upper-class academia had once before had reason to close ranks, some ninety years prior to the Davis–Sedgewick affair.

In the early afternoon of Sunday 27 February 1825 two gentlemen scholars became involved in a heated disagreement. The verbal exchange swiftly transcended into a physical one. Several blows were landed before the two antagonists were separated by a captain of the school. Honour, however, was not satisfied and both parties were agreeable to a pugilistic contest the following afternoon.

The combatants came from the finest aristocracy. The Hon. F. Ashley Cooper, aged fourteen or fifteen (reports vary), son of the Earl of Shaftesbury, was prepared to do battle with George Alexander Wood, sixteen or seventeen, son of Colonel Wood and nephew of the Marquis of Londonderry. The engagement commenced at 4 p.m. on Monday 28 February in Eton fields. The contestants, stripped to the waist, were ably encouraged by their brother scholars. It is reported that Mr Wood was some 6 inches the taller and by far the stronger boy, but his advantages were somewhat offset by Mr Cooper being far quicker and lighter on his feet.

Eton and its pupils, scene of the slaying of the Hon. F. Ashley Cooper

By round ten it was obvious that Mr Cooper's strength was failing. He was getting by far the worst of the engagement and although being knocked to the ground on several occasions had vowed never to give in.

Seeing the quickly worsening condition of their champion, Mr Cooper's seconds found it prudent to try to resurrect his flagging spirits by pouring copius quantities of brandy down his throat. Mr Wood's backers retaliated by adopting the same treatment for their mentor.

Stimulated now by cognac and heartened by the ever increasing euphoria of their colleagues, the two boys fought an incredible sixty rounds until well past six in the evening. It was at this time that Mr Cooper received a blow to the face that pitched him heavily upon his head. He lay there unconscious, unmoving.

The two brothers of the Hon. Ashley Cooper carried his inert body to his lodgings at the home of the Reverend Knapp. There he was put to bed, but surprisingly no medical assistance was obtained for some four hours. A short while afterwards the young man expired.

On 9 March 1825 Mr George Alexander Wood, aged approximately seventeen, and Mr Alexander Wellesley Leith, aged approximately thirteen, were charged with the unlawful slaying of the Hon. F. Ashley Cooper. The trial was at Aylesbury Assizes in front of Mr Justice Gaseler.

The proceedings were brief. Judge Gaseler had a short while previously directed the jury to find a prisoner not guilty through lack of evidence. He then turned his attention to the Cooper case.

The prisoners at the bar were joined by three well-known magistrates and local dignitaries. Lord Nugent, Colonel Browne and Sir John Dashwood-King stood beside the trembling boys in the dock, silently daring the prosecution to take further steps in what was, when all was said and done, a schoolboy fight, however tragic the outcome.

Mr Justice Gaseler turned to the prosecution and asked it to produce its witnesses. A Mr C. Teasdale, a Dr J. O'Reilly and servant Dorothy Large, were ready and available, but the prosecution in its wisdom decided to drop the case against the boys.

Mr Justice Gaseler instructed the jury that there was no case to answer and that they must return a verdict of not guilty. This they did and Wood and Leith, surrounded by many gentlemen of distinction, were returned to Eton.

Justice would have seemed to have been done. Possibly the verdict was right for all the wrong reasons. Both the *Reading Mercury* and *Berkshire Chronicle* were tacit and shared a reluctance to elucidate on the case. Both papers restricted their reports to a sympathetic paragraph or two describing 'Melancholy Events', 'Untimely Graves' and 'Noble Families'. Perhaps in hindsight these were genuine sentiments and the most practical way to conclude this lugubrious event.

There is one thing, however, that remains an enigma. Who in fact was Mr Alexander Wellesley Leith, aged thirteen, and what involvement did he have in the matter? The young gentleman's name does not appear until he is charged in court. There is no mention whatsoever of his being involved in the affray. We shall never know. I have scrutinized all the available documentation without the glimmer of a clue. No doubt he was of noble birth as were the majority of Eton scholars. Wellesley is the family name of the Duke of Wellington; perhaps young Alexander was extremely well connected. It is a point of conjecture.

CHAPTER TWO

A CRIME OF PASSION

In the 1850s Jon Carey kept a small inn at Warfield. It is little changed today, and stands just off the Bracknell Road. In Jon's time it was only an alehouse, patronized by a few locals. As with most alehouses in those days it was subsidized by various other endeavours. In Jon's case this meant a small farm.

Under this system the wife generally took care of the inn by day while the husband was employed on other duties. Then in the evening the man would look after the customers while his wife fixed meals and tended to the children.

Things went tolerably well for Jon Carey, his farm showed a relative profit, his young attractive wife (some fifteen years his junior at thirty-two) was popular in the bar, his children Alexander aged eleven and Charles aged four were bright and healthy.

Happiness for the Careys, however, was to be short-lived. An attractive lady meeting socially with people on a daily basis is vulnerable, especially when her hard-working, elderly husband is otherwise engaged.

Temptation appeared in the ruggedly masculine shape of George Parker. George was a popular fellow in the community, a farm labourer with a handsome face and a winning style. As with many affairs it was not a decision so much as an adjustment. George had just lost his wife and was devastated; he sought liquid solace in The Leathern Bottle and found Hannah Carey's shoulder to cry on.

Later, sympathy turned to affection, compassion turned to desire. Solace was found through sexual fulfilment. Jon Carey soon noticed a change in his wife. She was drinking a lot, short-tempered and unfair with the boys. Although she now always dressed in her limited finery, she was failing to fulfil his needs both sexually and nutritiously. Jon was often left to make his own meals after returning late from the fields. Jon Carey was not a fool, he realized that his wife had a lover and, soon after, that the lover was George Parker.

The slightly forbidding aspect of the new Leathern Bottle at Warfield, built on the site of the original; it was here that Hannah Carey met her fate

Strangely enough Carey suffered this state of affairs for five years. As time went by the affair was conducted less surreptitiously: it was an open secret. Hannah seemed to delight in throwing her indiscretions in Jon's face. On occasions the worm did turn, albeit ineffectively. One evening Carey demanded that Parker leave The Leathern Bottle and not return. Ignoring her irate husband Hannah calmly took down George's pewter pot and filled it with ale and handed it to him.

From then onwards there were frequent battles between Jon Carey and his wife, Hannah regularly sporting black eyes in the public bar. The fights culminated in a terrible bedroom scene with Carey beating his wife severely and then laying the bed upon her and jumping up and down on it. Despite pitiful pleas from his young son Charles, Carey's onslaught continued until, anger totally spent, he collapsed from sheer exhaustion on the floor. He stayed there all night holding the form of his much-loved Hannah.

In the morning Carey fetched Dr Thompson but he could do little for Hannah. She was barely alive. Esther Bruton her sister was fetched from Wokingham, she in turn notified John Wigg the Warfield constable. Hannah, however, survived between life and death for several weeks. Within that time she managed to recount her side of the story to Mr Harry, a local magistrate.

Hannah died of her injuries on 14 November 1851. She was laid to rest

Easthampstead church, where Hannah Carey was laid to rest in answer to her dying request beside her mother in Easthampstead churchyard. Her husband Jon was arrested the following day. He appeared before Baron Platt at Reading Assizes in February 1852.

In court Carey's fifteen-year-old son Alexander said that his mother drank a lot. He also stated that they were a happy family until Parker arrived on the scene. The jury found Carey guilty with a strong plea for leniency. Baron Platt gave out an extremely light sentence for that period of time: Carey was to be transported for seven years. Even this was not light enough for Carey, who pleaded not to be sent out of the country for his sons' sake, but Baron Platt would not be moved.

CHAPTER THREE

THE BOYN HILL TRAGEDY

In 1850 Isaac Lee, a successful London businessman, had a breakdown. Life was perfect until his wife died; they had been a devoted couple, but now late in his life Isaac found himself frighteningly alone. Lee was lodged in Bedlam, the London hospital for the insane, the word insane at that time covering a multitude of ailments from mild depression to raving lunacy.

Isaac was released on licence to his sister and her husband, John and

Hogarth's interpretation of Bedlam, where Isaac Lee was incarcerated both before and after the Boyn Hill Tragedy

Elizabeth Cannon of Boyn Hill, Maidenhead. Things went well for a couple of years, Isaac Lee enjoying the company and John and Elizabeth not disenchanted by the money provided by their affluent relative. Soon, however, cracks appeared in Isaac's mental stability. Small things at first, just little things that needed keeping an eye on.

In spring 1852 little Lizzie Cannon was staying with her grandparents John and Elizabeth. Lizzie was a playful and popular four-year-old, well loved by the small community. Unfortunately Lizzie was left alone with Isaac in the kitchen when a young piglet ran into the room. For no apparent reason the old man went crazy with rage and picking up a billhook he smashed the animal across the head, snapping its jaws. He then chased its squealing retreat into the kitchen. Isaac aimed another blow but missed completely.

By this time young Lizzie had made for the old man with arms raised in protest. The fire of madness was in Isaac's eyes as he brought the blade down again and again on the little girl's head. There were screams and then silence as the tiny body, deprived of life, slid to the floor.

Isaac Lee seemed to be in limbo, but on seeing the village constable John Frewin approaching his insanity reared once more and he fought with a frenzy belying his years. It took four men to contain and handcuff the old man as he struggled like a man possessed.

Lee was remanded in Reading, while a coroner's jury recorded a case of wilful murder against him. Lee was found unfit to plead and returned to Bedlam. A shocked little community returned to their homes, but the 'Boyn Hill Tragedy' was spoken of in hushed voices for many years.

CHAPTER FOUR

ROSA ROSE ACCUSED OF WILFUL MURDER OF HER CHILD

Rosa Rose, an attractive girl of twenty-six, gave birth to her second illegitimate child in early December 1869. It had been a hard and painful birth. Rosa was at the time staying with Mrs Emily Hearne and her daughter at 27 Church Street, Reading.

Mrs Hearne, a widow, had known Rosa for some half a dozen years. She was fond of her, and her daughter Alice thought the world of the cheerful if promiscuous young madam.

On 10 December the caring widow accompanied Rosa to have the child John Rose registered. Rosa had grown painfully thin and had never actually recovered from the traumatic birth. On 16 December, a wet and blustery day, Rosa set out to visit her mother in Warfield some 12 miles from Reading in the direction of Windsor. She had intimated to Mrs Hearne that she would be staying with her mother for the foreseeable future. This surprised the widow as she knew that Rosa had never been on good terms with her mother, and with the disgrace of a second come-by-chance Mrs Rose had erupted and shown her daughter the door. Mrs Hearne hoped there had been a reconciliation; much as she liked the girl, Rosa was an unpaid guest and now with the child she was even more hard work. Emily Hearne trusted that the reconciliation would be a long one. She waved goodbye with a guarded air of relief.

On Friday 17 December Emily Hearne was working in a house near her home in Church Street, Reading. She was a qualified nurse and she was tending one of the children of a local businessman. Looking up from her charge she was surprised to observe her daughter Alice racing down the street towards her. The slim thirteen-year-old was in a greatly distressed condition. As her mother opened the door Alice blurted between sobs, 'Come Mummy, little Johnny is dead – Rosa is at our house.'

The sight that met Emily Hearne at home was distressing indeed. Rosa stood in the hall motionless, the tiny body of Johnny in her arms. She was drenched to the skin and the tiny infant's body was wrapped in a shawl so wet that the water still ran from the end of the garment.

After ascertaining that the tiny form was lifeless Mrs Hearne sent straight away for a surgeon who lived nearby. Mr Muggeridge arrived within minutes, and the body was examined with speed and efficiency. Mr Muggeridge felt and listened to the lungs. 'I believe', he said, 'that this child has been immersed in water. If I'm not mistaken this infant has been drowned.' (This statement was later confirmed by a post-mortem.) 'I know,' replied Rosa, 'I fell in a ditch with him last night.'

Mr Muggeridge, suspicious of the circumstances, informed the Reading police. Rosa Rose was arrested by Inspector Townsend and conveyed to the town police station where she was remanded. Rosa was in a very poorly condition, she had not eaten the day before, her lungs were congested and she had a terrible cough. It was also rumoured that she still had complications from the birth of Johnny. It was a very sick and shivering young woman who was conveyed to the hospital quarters of Reading's gaunt gaol.

On 27 December Rosa Rose was remanded for one week. She was deemed too ill to attend the hearing. On 4 January 1870 there was a further remand, Rosa still being too ill to appear. Finally, on 23 January a hearing was held within the walls of Reading Gaol. In the specifically designated justice room evidence was placed before magistrates Mr Leveson-Gower and Mr W.T. Bridges.

Emily Hearne and her daughter Alice stated that Rosa had left them to travel to Warfield on Thursday 16 December, returning in a pitiful condition with the deceased child on Friday 17 December. Mr Muggeridge gave some highly specialized observations and with evidence from him, the doctor who had carried out the autopsy and the Reading coroner, it was proved beyond doubt that little John Rose had expired through drowning. There next followed a long and detailed account of the missing twenty-four hours by the accused. Looking extremely frail Rosa was permitted to give evidence while seated. A precise account of a rather contradictory statement was made as follows.

Rosa had set out on Thursday 16 December with baby John to visit her mother at Warfield. She discovered that she could not afford the coach fare

The Stag and Hounds at Binfield, where the bedraggled Rosa Rose stopped for sustenance prior to the death of her baby John. (Photograph by P. Bourne)

and had decided to walk there. This was quite ambitious for a sick girl with an eleven-day-old child in inclement weather. Rosa had passed through Binfield about 4.30, stopping off at The Stag and Hounds to dry herself out and purchase some liquid refreshment. She had then continued to Warfield, a matter of some 1½ miles, but she got lost in the dark and overcome by fatigue she sought shelter in a wooden hut after falling in a ditch with the baby.

Being exhausted and drenched to the skin Rosa had lain inside the hut for most of the night. She stated, 'I think I could hear the baby murmuring outside the shed but I could not be sure. I was too exhausted to move.' The hearing deemed this a very strange statement indeed. Rosa deposed that she had awoken totally saturated. On examining the baby she suspected it to be dead, she had panicked and had tried to run for help with the baby in her arms. Her sodden petticoat had tripped her and she had fallen into another ditch. She discarded the offending petticoat and had walked the 12 miles back to Reading to Mrs Hearne. The rest of her story could be verified by Mrs Hearne, her daughter Alice and Mr Muggeridge.

Mr Leveson-Gower enquired as to whether or not Rosa had met her mother that day. After much hesitation the accused answered in the negative. Leveson-Gower then asked why, when she suspected the child to be dead, she had not gone on a few hundred yards to her mother's house rather than traipsing the dozen or so miles back to Reading. Rosa explained a little unconvincingly that she was distressed and looked upon Mrs Hearne as her mother and Mrs Hearne's family as her family.

Here ended Rosa Rose's testimony. Evidence was then given by Mrs Harriet Roberts, landlady of The Stag and Hounds at Binfield. She stated that a young lady, whom she recognized as the accused, had called at her inn late in the afternoon of Thursday 16 December. The young lady was accompanied by a baby and they were both thoroughly soaked to the skin. The accused ordered brandy but Mrs Roberts had convinced her that hot tea would be more beneficial. She had drunk the tea and left despite protestation from the landlady that she should remain and dry herself.

Mrs Roberts had watched the young lady cross the bridge over the Ry on the Warfield Road. She had also noticed her return the same way the following morning.

George Lamb, a gardener, then gave evidence. He stated that he had seen a young girl whom he now recognized to be the accused in the early evening of 16 December at the gate of Mrs Rose's house in Warfield. The girl was carrying a bundle and seemed greatly distressed. He asked if she was scared of the dogs that were doing a good deal of barking. She replied that she wasn't and walked away. The following morning Mr Lamb had discovered a petticoat partially buried in a nearby wood.

Lamb was followed in evidence by Police Sergeant Blake, who stated that he had returned with Lamb to the spot where the gardener had found the petticoat. He had measured the distances and had found it 180 yards from Mrs Rose's house and 80 yards from the nearest footpath.

Inspector Townsend gave evidence of arrest and stated that the accused kept repeating the same sentence: 'Me and Johnny fell in a ditch and he drowned.' He had taken the accused to Reading borough police station where she was charged. She was placed in the hands of Mrs Purchase, the chief superintendent's wife, who proceeded to search her. Mrs Purchase stated that she had searched Rosa's pockets and found some wet linen, some brown paper, string and 19s and 11d in change. Mrs Purchase was the last to give evidence. Mr Bridges and Mr Leveson-Gower considered all the statements and evidence. They decided that there was an indictment to answer and Rosa was remanded to the assizes on 25 February 1870 charged with the wilful murder of her baby.

Poor Rosa Rose, had she accidentally drowned her baby while struggling to extricate herself from a flood-soaked ditch, or had she of her own volition deliberately immersed the infant with intent to kill? Only Rosa knew the truth.

The grand jury, meeting at Reading under Mr Justice Hanson, obviously believed her. At the Lent Assizes they ignored the bill of indictment. Rosa Rose walked free without a word of evidence being heard, the general consensus of opinion being that she was a rather lucky young lady. The evidence at Reading Gaol had been inundated with inconsistencies and contradictions, the greatest and most controversial being the contents of her pockets.

First the 19s and 11d (fractionally less than £1): in 1870 the average wage of a skilled labourer was about £15 a year. The coach trip from Reading to Warfield would have cost about 1s (5 pence). Why should a lady trudge some 12 miles in the pouring rain with a baby when she could afford to sit comfortably in a coach?

The same thing applied at The Stag and Hounds. Rosa had sufficient for a warm meal for herself and something for the baby. Why sit there with just a cup of tea, especially when she was drenched and rain was teeming down outside.

Also, even if Rosa's mother had turned her away there were several cheap inns a few hundred yards away in Warfield, or The Stag and Hounds not far back along the Reading Road. Was she so exhausted that she could make it to none of these?

Strange also was Rosa's evidence, 'I think I could hear the baby murmuring outside the shed.' Are we really to believe that she spent the night inside the shed with the baby outside in the pouring rain? Too exhausted to pull the tiny infant in, and yet a few hours later this same lady finds the energy to carry the tiny body back to Reading over 10 miles away.

Second, and just as criminally indicting, the brown paper and string, two articles which have been synonymous with the disposal of tiny cadavers for years. Hardly an infant's body was found in the country without its being wrapped in brown paper and tied with string for decency's sake. It was this Victorian habit of putting everything in respectable wrappings that had brought about the downfall of Mrs Amelia Dyer, the notorious Reading baby-farmer, when her name and address were found on the paper surrounding one of her murdered chargelings.

Why did Rosa possess the brown paper and string, what did she intend to use them for? These were questions she refused to answer at the hearing. Questions Inspector Townsend would dearly have loved the opportunity of asking in court.

Of course it is possible that Rosa had used the paper and string for packing spare garments when leaving Reading, but Mrs Hearne certainly didn't notice her leave with a parcel. It is also possible that Rosa walked to Warfield because she had no money at the time. If this was the case where did she obtain the 19s 11d? Had she in fact met her mother, despite her denial? Had she then been sent packing but with £1? Had George Lamb been mistaken and was Rosa not approaching her mother's but leaving with the dogs set upon her? Mrs Rose was a very respectable and upright woman. So much so that she refused to appear at the hearing. Had she done so a lot of questions might have been answered.

However, she didn't and the speculative variations remain endless. Only Rosa knew.

CHAPTER FIVE

THE MURDER OF MRS E. REVILLE, WIFE OF A SLOUGH BUTCHER, APRIL 1881

Mrs Reville ran a small butcher's shop with her husband Hesekiah in Windsor Road, Slough. The pair employed two apprentices, Phillip Glass, a lad of fourteen, and Alfred Payne, a lad of sixteen. Both young men had been with the firm for approximately two years.

For several months now Hesekiah had been worried; meat had been disappearing from the shop at an alarming rate. He and his wife suspected Payne, they had heard rumours of meat being sold off cheap outside The Royal Oak, a hostelry run by Payne's father. Mr Reville and his wife had taken opposite stands on the matter. Mrs Reville had been for sacking Payne out of hand but Hesekiah was all for having absolute proof before taking any action that might lead to embarrassment. Payne's father was, when all was said and done, a fellow business man of the town.

It was with the end-view of finding some proof that Mr Reville had approached Mrs Glass, the mother of his other apprentice. Relying on her integrity he had asked her to find out from Phillip how Payne was smuggling joints out of the shop. He pointed out to Mrs Glass that there was now a smouldering war of attrition between Mrs Reville and Payne. There was an atmosphere in his shop and he must get to the bottom of the thieving for everybody's sake. Assuring him of her secrecy Mrs Glass bade her son's employer good night.

On Monday 11 April 1881 at 6.30 Mr Reville was enjoying a noggin at his local. At his nearby shop Mrs Reville was in the back doing the accounts while the two apprentices were making ready for the following day. They were washing down counters, Payne with the fervour adopted by a man who has been wrongly accused of some misdemeanour. He worked sullenly and petulantly with an application recently inflamed by scornful words from his employer's wife.

At 6.30 Phillip Glass left for his home, leaving his comrade behind to rub ham for the morning. At 8.30 George Roll, a bricklayer walking home, greeted Payne outside the shop. Roll was later to describe Payne as agitated and in a hurry to get away. At 8.35 Kate Timms met Alfred Payne hurrying along the High Street.

At 8.45 a friend, Mrs Beasley, called on Mrs Reville. Mrs Beasley discovered her friend lying dead in her chair with extensive and horrifying wounds to her head and neck. Mr Dodd, a local surgeon, arrived to inspect the body and shortly after, a distraught Hesekiah Reville arrived after being contacted at the local pub; with him was Sergeant Hobbs of the Slough Police.

At 9.20 Superintendent Dunham arrived, a very astute and formidable officer. Some three years previously he had brought a sevenfold killer to justice at Denham.

The obvious weapon, a meat cleaver, was lying beside the body. As far as the distraught Mr Reville could ascertain there had been nothing taken. Robbery was certainly not the motive. As Mr Dodd lifted the bloodied weapon, what purported to be the motive lay underneath in the form of a piece of notepaper. Superintendent Dunham lifted the blood-soaked note and read: 'I have done this because you sold me some bad meat on Saturday to my family. You won't sell them no more bad meat. Mr Collins, Colnbrook.'

Superintendent Dunham asked Reville if he had a customer named Collins at Colnbrook. The butcher replied in the affirmative but denied ever selling him bad meat. As far as he knew he was still on the best terms with Mr Collins. Also that was not Collins's writing nor would he use such a semi-literate style.

After hearing evidence about the pilfering from the shop and the smouldering atmosphere between Payne and Mrs Reville, Dunham was of a single mind as to who had perpetrated this heinous crime. He did not undervalue the element of surprise. Payne was apprehended at The Royal Oak and conveyed to Slough police station late that same evening.

There he was requested to write his name and various other trivia. When informed about the murder he dogmatically repeated that Mrs Reville had been alive and well when he had left at 8.30.

On 16 April Payne was taken before Mr Springwell-Johnson Esq. and remanded until the petty sessions. Two days later the coroner's court opened; its venue was the Crown Inn, the coroner Mr Charsley. Evidence concerning the pilfering was heard from Hesekiah Reville, Mrs Glass and her son, and also evidence of the rows and the atmosphere between the deceased and Payne. Evidence that Payne had left the shop at 8.30 was offered by Mr George Roll and Mrs Kate Timms. Incidentally his time of leaving the shop had never been denied by Payne.

An emotional Mrs Beasley described the discovery of her friend's body. Sergeant Hobbs gave confirming evidence. Mr Dodd gave a lengthy account of the poor woman's injuries, most of which was confirmed and established by Mr Buee, the police surgeon.

Superintendent Dunham was on the stand for some time. With a surgeon's precision he did a clinical assassination of Alfred Payne, from the motive through the opportunity to the mass of circumstantial evidence. He described the murder note as laughable but informed the court that just to be on the safe side he had interviewed Collins and found him to have a cast-iron alibi.

Dunham also had some surprises; he had found that the unlikely and

Slough High Street, a few years after the tragic slaying of Mrs E. Reville
(photograph by courtesy of Berkshire County Library)

preposterous confession purporting to be from Collins had actually been written on paper torn from a notebook owned by Payne. The half-sheet of paper fitted exactly the half-sheet remaining in the book. When Dunham sat down Mr Charles Chabot, a handwriting expert, was called. The mild and polite Chabot requested a recess. He informed the coroner that more examples of Payne's handwriting had been received by him and he would need time to study them. He intended there to be no mistake in a matter as grave as this.

Mr Charsley granted the request. When Chabot returned after a two-hour adjournment he had some devastating observations to relate. To a hushed court he stated that he had found at least fifteen similarities between Payne's writing and the alleged confession of Collins. When asked by the coroner if he were sure that the examples and the confession had been written by the same hand Chabot replied that his was not an exact science but he had never seen so many similarities in two examples. He was as certain as it was possible to be that the writer of the confession was one and the same as the writer of the other notes. Chabot then took his seat.

Alfred Payne was on the stand but briefly. As dogmatic as ever he repeated that Mrs Reville and himself were on good terms, she was alive and well when he left her and nothing on God's earth would make him say otherwise. If they were looking for a murder why didn't they question some of the many tramps that infested the area.

Payne's observation was correct as far as it went, there was a collection of lean-tos around the corner from the shop that was absolutely festooned with gentlemen of the road. As far as the police were concerned, however, this was a non-starter. A self-respecting tramp would at least have stolen something from the premises.

Dunham knew he had Payne dead to rights. It was no surprise when the jury returned a verdict of wilful murder against the prisoner. Alfred Payne was conveyed to Aylesbury to await trial at the assizes.

As Superintendent Dunham approached the assize court at Aylesbury on 28 April 1881 he must have been as confident as any police officer on any similar occasion. He had the motive: thieving and fear of dismissal. He had the opportunity as Payne had been left alone with Mrs Reville for nearly two hours. He had the strong circumstantial evidence of the page from Payne's notebook and he had Chabot, the country's leading handwriting expert, willing to testify that Payne had written the Collins confession in a pathetic attempt to put the police on the wrong track.

After a three-day trial, the only evidence for the defence was the small loophole that it was possible, just barely possible, that in the short time between Payne leaving at 8.30 and Mrs Beasley discovering the body at 8.45 somebody had the opportunity to enter and leave the premises. On this unbelievably slender chance in a million the jury acquitted Alfred Payne.

Why? the papers wanted to know. How could it be? asked the public. Nods of bewilderment and disbelief from the prosecution and police. If Alfred Payne didn't do it, who did? Who else could it possibly have been? There was of course no answer.

The case remained open officially as far as Slough Police were concerned. To Dunham, Payne was as guilty as Judas. He made no further enquiries. How then can one explain the jury's verdict faced with such an overwhelming mass of proof?

One cannot explain it but one can offer an explanation. In 1881 if a person was found guilty of murder that person was hanged. The judge was granted no leeway, no choice. There was no appeal system, as sure as night followed day a guilty verdict was followed by a preordained death sentence. This was intended to act as a deterrent but it sometimes had an adverse effect on justice. Juries realizing the inevitable outcome of a guilty verdict would fly in the face of logic, reason and overwhelming evidence and acquit an accused man, purely and simply out of pity. It is possible the jury in the Alfred Payne case looked at this sixteen-year-old youth and ignored both the letter and the spirit of the law. At the risk of being a bore, 'The quality of mercy is not strained. It droppeth . . . '

CHAPTER SIX

THE MURDER OF CHARLES DANCE, A CHALVEY COAL MERCHANT

In 1888 the village of Chalvey was just independent of Slough. Its geographical position, its close proximity, made it inevitable that it would soon be engulfed by its insatiable neighbour. In the late 1880s, however, it remained a village with its village characteristics, its gossip and characters marking it apart from the unobtrusive mundanity of a much larger metropolis.

It was nearing Christmas, 22 December. Charles Dance, a middle-aged coal dealer, was making ready to pick up his club money from The Garibaldi. Charles lived with his wife next door to The Foresters Arms at the centre of Chalvey. He rented the premises from a Mr Hines and employed one full-time worker, a man named Higgins, and some seasonal part-time help.

It was Higgins who had been asked by his employer to call for him at 8 p.m. and to accompany him to The Garibaldi. This Higgins had done but without success, being informed by Mrs Dance that her husband had left earlier to tend to some business.

Charles Dance was vulnerable; he carried vast amounts of money about with him, sometimes in excess of £20. He was known to carry this in a small black saddle bag that was his constant companion. He frequently patrolled most of the local hostelries, for this was the way he did business. In fact the night before, he had collected nearly £7 from Elizabeth Darling at The Rising Sun for a season's coal.

It was just after Higgins had left that Mrs Dance was interrupted for a second time. She opened the window to see a local man, William James, standing below. 'Charles,' he was shouting, 'Uncle Charles. There's a man looking for you.' 'Mr Dance is not here', Amelia Dance retorted. She did not like James; few people did. Charles was not his uncle and she disliked young men who were over-familiar with their elders. James had worked for them at odd times but had been shiftless and thoroughly dishonest. In fact ducks and other edible fowl had been disappearing from the little small-holding the Dances ran behind their coal business. It had got so bad that they had informed PC Horne, who in turn had found James sleeping in a shed where Dance kept his tools. Also he had discovered down feathers in a box at the quarry where James worked. This was in the previous November. Charles had decided not to press charges but now they were losing chickens again and her husband was doing the occasional night-time vigil.

'Will you tell uncle Charles when he comes back that this gentleman will see him at Hines',' (The Foresters Arms). Mrs Dance looked into the night. She could make out James's silhouette but could not see a figure beside him. 'Try The Garibaldi', she shouted curtly and closed the window.

William James was later to state on oath that he had left Mrs Moody's, where he lodged, at 8 o'clock. He had gone to the laundry where his mother worked and chatted to her for several minutes, he had then continued around Bird's Eye Corner and met a man who had enquired after Charles Dance. He described the man as about forty years of age, dressed in an overcoat and a soft felt hat, about 5 feet 4 inches in height and sporting dark side-whiskers. He had also been accompanied by a dog. James had seen the man before in both Eton and Slough. After escorting him to Dance's yard and enquiring unsuccessfully of Dance's whereabouts he had left the man's company. This man was never traced.

Mrs Sarah Jane Moody was James's landlady. The young man owed her 8s for four weeks' rent. She had had a go at him on Tuesday 19 December and he had promised her the money on Friday. It was now Friday at 6.10 p.m. and James was about to go out so the landlady thought it prudent to breach the subject yet again. 'Don't worry about the money, Mrs Moody', her lodger replied. 'I am drawing my Christmas money from The White Hart tonight, you will be paid in full.' Mrs Moody would have to be satisfied with that for the time being.

William James left the house at 6.15 but returned at 7.50 in an agitated state. He came into the living room and took off his jacket. He then removed his boots and placed them on the open fire. Turning to Mrs Moody he stated, 'Just tell anybody that asks that I didn't go out till after 8.' He washed briefly, grabbed an old coat from his room and then left the house. At 10.10 James returned again to his lodgings and was met by Mrs Moody and her husband. The Moodys had anticipated having a little trouble with extracting the rent but James handed over 1s 6d saying that The White Hart had paid him some 30s but he had drunk some of it with 'Whoops My Darlin' (the nickname of the local lady of easy virtue). He intended to break a 10s note in the morning and pay the remainder. A deal was struck and William James retired for the night.

By 10.30 p.m. on Friday 22 December Mrs Dance was beginning to get a little anxious about her husband, it was not like him to be late. The worry turned into a nagging doubt by 11 p.m. so the good lady awakened Higgins. He in turn promised to traipse round the local Slough and Chalvey pubs with the hope of contacting his employer. By 11.45 Higgins had returned without success. He pointed out that all the pubs had been closed for some time and went on in an attempt to console Mrs Dance by saying that it was Christmas and her husband had numerous business associates in the town with whom he might be enjoyin a late noggin. Far from reassured Mrs Dance bade Higgins good night.

It was a very worried woman that knocked on Higgins's door at 5 a.m. on 23 December. She begged him to continue the search but Higgins's assignment was brief and horrifyingly productive. He shone his torch on Dance's tool shed door, and there was what appeared to be a black substance on the handle. Higgins dabbed his finger on the substance and held it up, its texture immediately informing him that it was blood. The torch beam traversed the half-acre of small-holding. There staring into space was the expressionless face of Charles Dance, his features beaten virtually beyond recognition. The lifeless form was lain over an upturned wheelbarrow, the victim having been ferociously beaten and obviously dragged from the shed. The money bag was missing.

Higgins apprehended a passing paper boy and sent him for the police. Careful not to touch anything, he opened the door of the small coal office. It was now his unenviable task to inform Mrs Dance.

The inquest opened on the same morning, Saturday 23 December. Mr Charsley, the coroner, presided at the Cape of Good Hope inn. Higgins and Mrs Dance gave evidence followed by William Urban Buee, the police surgeon. Mr Buee described the unfortunate man's injuries: there was a severe wound on the mouth, the jaw was broken and the cheek torn open exposing a 2 inch gap of flesh. The corpse had a cut hand and a broken finger where he had obviously tried to protect himself. The blows had been caused by a sledgehammer or something similar. There was also a fractured skull and a tremendous loss of blood from the blow to the face. There were contusions to the neck where something had been pulled tight about the throat. It was Mr Buee's considered opinion, however, that the victim had choked to death on his own blood. Mr Charsley thanked the surgeon for his evidence and adjourned the inquiry until Friday 29 December.

Superintendent Dunham arrested William Alfred James on Sunday 24 December. James was brought before Mr Springwell-Johnson and remanded until Wednesday's petty sessions where a preliminary examination would take place.

On Wednesday 27 December the prisoner was examined before Mr Springwell-Johnson, Captain Higgins, Mr E.C. Secker and Mr Thomas Mosley. Mrs Sarah Jane Moody was on the stand for over two hours. She told of James's suspicious actions on the night of 22 December, of his going out at 6.15 and his returning at 7.50, of his burning his boots and changing his jacket, which was later found to be blood-stained, of his warning her to witness that he had not gone out before 8 o'clock, of his washing and of the money he had somehow procured (when he paid her the 1s 6d she had noticed that he had several notes in his possession).

Mrs Moody brought forward fresh evidence strongly substantiated by her neighbours. She told of blood in the sink where James had been washing, of blood in the drains outside that she and a neighbour had sluiced away with buckets of water.

There before a massive, but hushed crowd at Slough she told of the following Saturday morning. James had gone out early and returned about 10 a.m. to find Mrs Moody and her neighbour washing down the drains. 'What have you been doing, chittlings?' he enquired in a flippant manner. He then went on to inform them that old Dance was dead and that the police had picked up his jacket. Turning to Mrs Moody he had pointed straight at her and emphasized, 'Remember I did not go out till after 8.' He also seemed worried that he had lost his white belt the night before. Mrs Moody then provided him with an old necktie to keep up his trousers. After this evidence the inquiry was adjourned for several days.

The following day Mr Charles Dance was laid to rest. His coffin was flanked by an immense number of mourners.

The hearing resumed on the Friday. Mr Brumwell-Smith for the prosecution re-called Sarah Jane Moody. Much of her damning evidence was repeated. She described in much detail wet bloodstains she had discovered on James's coat and trousers and also specks of the same on the sink and the towel he had used. Once again proceedings were adjourned. The prosecution was waiting for forensic tests on James's clothing and various other articles.

When the evidence came (on Wednesday 9 January) it was inconclusive. Mr W.W. Fisher, public analyst for Berkshire, Buckinghamshire and Oxfordshire, stated that he had taken samples from a hat, coat, trousers, towel and money bag provided by Superintendent Dunham. There were definitely bloodstains on the coat and trousers but the clothes had been thoroughly washed and it was impossible to tell whether the stains had been human or animal blood.

Help came for James, albeit as a token gesture, when Mr Bull, a surgeon of Chelvey, testified that James had injured his wrist earlier that week and he did not deem it sufficiently healed for him to do such damage with a sledgehammer. Mr Bull was followed by Mr Seymour of Chalvey gravel pits. Seymour was James's employer and his evidence was swift and exact. William James worked for him spasmodically and was paid 2s 6d per day.

Superintendent Dunham then took the stand before a hushed court. The officer was a legend in his own lifetime. His meticulous and inexhaustible penchant for detail had made him a greatly respected member of the force. Dunham described the discovery of the body and the chain of events that led him to arrest James. He had no doubt that the murder had taken place in the shed and the body had been dragged outside. The very same shed that James had surreptitiously slept in on numerous occasions. A shed on a small-holding containing many fowl, birds which James had been suspected of stealing.

Dunham went on to elucidate an interview he had had with James on the afternoon of 23 December. James had assured him that he did not go out until 8 o'clock on 22 December but he (Dunham) had found this to be totally untrue when he had subsequently interviewed Mrs Moody. Dunham did not wish to elaborate on this as the magistrates had already heard this evidence from the good lady's testimony. There were, however, others who would shortly endorse Mrs Moody's words. With these words the superintendent sat down.

The next three witnesses were as brief as they were fatalistic. Thomas Austin, a gardener, described how he had met James at 7.20 on the night of 22 December. James had borrowed 2d off him as he claimed he hadn't the price of a pint. William James, who was making a pathetic job of conducting his own defence, cross-examined the witness. 'Are you sure it was 7.20 and not 8.20 when we met?' 'Quite sure,' came the reply, 'I was home indoors by 7.45.'

Austin was followed on to the stand by James Prudence Catherwood, landlord of The White Hart. He deposed that James certainly hadn't drawn any money from his slate club on 22 December. The prisoner had been a member but had defaulted in April, drawing out the meagre pittance he had managed to accumulate.

Even more damning evidence arrived in the personage of James Henry Swain of Rose Cottage, High Street, Chalvey. He had been out walking his dog near The Foresters Arms on Friday 22 December at 7.35 p.m. He had seen a tall slender man climb the fence at Dance's coal yard. The man fitted James's description in every particular. When asked why he hadn't reported the matter to the police Swain replied that he had thought it was some poor bloke after a chicken for Christmas. On being shown James's coat Swain stated that he was convinced that it was one and the same as that worn by the man he'd seen climbing the fence. After this deposition Swain returned to his seat.

The final witness was yet another publican, Alfred Glass of The Flags public house. Glass stated that James had arrived at about 8.10 p.m. He was drinking porter and strong ale. At 8.30 James was joined by a lady of suspect virtue known as 'Whoops My Darlin'. Mr Springwell-Johnson asked the lady's correct name but Mr Glass said he did not know, she had simply been known as 'Whoops My Darlin' for a number of years.

Alfred Glass continued to describe how James had plied the lady with Irish whiskey and porter ale. To a question from the bench Glass replied that in all he estimated that James had spent between 6s and 7s. Glass reflected that at the time he had wondered why the young man had invested so heavily when in the past he had known others achieve their ambition

The Flags public house at Chalvey, where William James and 'Whoops My Darlin'
enjoyed drinks on the fateful night of Friday 22 December 1888. (Photograph by
P. Bourne)

with a mere fraction of this expense. There was laughter in the court but
Springwell-Johnson took a dim view of it. He reminded Glass that he was
here to give evidence, not for speculation or observations, and as there
were no more questions perhaps he would be good enough to stand down.

The jury returned a verdict of wilful murder against William James. He
was remanded in custody to appear at the assizes.

William James stood trial on 2 February 1889 at Aylesbury Assizes.
Judge Sir James Fitzjames-Stephens presided. Bonsley and Percival-Keep
were for the prosecution, Attenborough and Lindell for the defence. James
was said to be nonchalant and confident. The most surprising piece of
evidence was thrust upon the jury at the eleventh hour. Mr Attenborough
produced Ann Stanley and her husband James. Ann Stanley, a thirty-year-
old housewife, testified under oath that William James had brought to her
two fowl at 7.30 p.m. on 22 December. She had paid James for those birds

and others she had received from him previously. On 22 December, she continued, James had obviously been poaching; there was blood on his hands and jacket. James Stanley stated that he had returned home at 8 p.m. and seen the aforementioned fowl on his draining board.

This was startling new evidence. All the rest of the attestation had been thoroughly turned over at the minor hearings. There was, however, a little fresh evidence from Mr Bull the local surgeon. It had been proved that Mr Dance's body had been dragged several yards by some type of rope or harness (James had lost his belt). Under cross-examination Mr Bull deposed that it would be absolutely impossible for a man with an injured wrist, such as James had, to drag a heavy body some half a dozen yards.

Mr Attenborough KC, the most eminent and wily of lawyers, based the whole of his defence address on the somewhat suspect and felicitous testimony of the Stanleys. He stated that he could find a plausible answer for every suspicious action made by the prisoner. If one bore in mind that James had been poaching, everything fell into place.

Attenborough pointed out that on the night of 22 December James had been stealing fowls. This James would readily admit; but they were not Mr Dance's fowls for there were none missing. Of course he had blood on his hands, he'd been killing chickens. Would he not wash it off at home? Naturally he had told Mrs Moody to say he had not gone out until 8 p.m. The birds were probably purloined at 7 p.m. and sold to the Stanleys within half an hour. This also explained the burning of the boots, which might well have had tell-tale signs upon them. Would this poaching not also account for the money? When James met Thomas Austin at 7.20 that evening he had not the price of a pint, simply because he had not at that time been paid by Ann Stanley. Later, obviously he had money to spend on the lady at The Flags. Also he had told Mrs Moody that he was expecting money from The White Hart slate club. Obviously untrue, but he could hardly be expected to tell this respectable lady that he was about to be paid for stolen birds.

Attenborough went on to inform the jury that the only other evidence against his client was the sighting of a tall man climbing Dance's fence. This allegation was made by James Swain, a gentleman walking his dog. Surely it had been difficult on that dark, moonless, rainswept night to

Chalvey High Street a few years after the tragic murder of Charles Dance, the neighbourhood coal merchant. (Photograph by courtesy of Berkshire County Library)

identify one specific figure. There were many young men of James's build and stature.

With the court's full attention Attenborough exploited the logic of the case against his client. Was it likely that a man would commit a murder, then invent a stranger? Then walk with that imaginary stranger back to the scene of the crime and stand there shouting up at the window to attract attention to himself? After this extraordinary affair, was it believable that James stole some chickens and calmly walked to Ann Stanley's house, obtained payment, returned home, changed his clothes and went out to a pub? The jury thought not. William James was acquitted. He turned to the prosecution and exclaimed, 'Well you brought a rope but you couldn't hang me.' He then left the court, cordially shook hands with his many supporters and made for the nearest inn supported by those same well-wishers.

So James had been found not guilty. It has long been a criticism of British justice that a man is not convicted or acquitted by the facts, but by the verbal dexterity of the man presenting those facts. The James case was a classic example; he was saved by an exceptionally brilliant advocate, and a most unexpected felicitous deposition from the Stanleys. How ingeniously opportune. Take away the extremely suspect testimony of the Stanleys and James would have been, to coin a phrase, 'bang to rights'.

Reading between the lines of local newspapers, they and the people they represented were far from satisfied by the outcome of the case. The *Slough Observer* stated, with obvious sarcasm, that the police would continue their enquiries and they were sure that William James would help them in this matter to the utmost of his powers.

CHAPTER SEVEN

THE MURDER OF KATE LAURA DUNGEY AT LAMBRIDGE WOOD FARMHOUSE, NORTH OF HENLEY

'Don't mind if I do, sir, strong ale thank you. George Dawson's the name, and you're the chap wants to know about the murder are you? Well we ain't had a murder for years in Henley. Mary Blandy, her was the last. Poisoned her old father back in the 1750s. Well the one you're on about were a woman of thirty odd, she were found beat to death at Lambridge Wood Farm during December 1893. Yep, I was foreman there at the time, and coach driver too. It were a bad old do, her being so respectable and all, and meeting such a terrible death. They pulled in m'brother-in-law Walter Rathall, bloody fool. Me and Walter married two sisters, Welsh gals they was. Well 'ereford, near enough, sir. Do what, sir? Put events in order? Right, I'll start agen.

'Lambridge Wood House is at Assendon, just north of Henley, me and Walter grew up in the village. Well in the early '80s, this big tradesman from London, Mr Mash, took Lambridge Wood. It's called a farm but there weren't a lot of farming went on, he just sort of took it as a country retreat, but it were a bit remote for him so he took another gaff at New Street down in the town, there being more going on down there like. Well he ran the two places with his wife and kids. In 1882, soon after Mr Mash arrived, I applied for the job of farm foreman and coach driver. I got the job too, it were a doddle. I got old Mother Rathall a job up there too, you know Walter's mam. What with her being family and all, just a bit of cleaning and dusting around, but her enjoyed it, she were there five years, from 1882 to 1887. Walter, well Walter were always a-visiting, that's what done him the harm later on don't you see, but still, time enough for that later.

'Well then Mr Mash brings down this young woman, Kate Laura Dungey, twenty-three she were then and pretty as a picture. Straight-laced tho', no muckin', refined don't you know. Well first her's a governess to

Cottages at Assendon, the tiny hamlet near Henley, which was the home of both Walter Rathall and his brother-in-law George Dawson. (Photograph by P. Bourne)

Mash's two daughters, let's see, her done that job till, let me see, about 1890, yeah, about four years, but then what with the girls getting in their teens and that and spending more time in London, well her warn't needed you see, not in that capacity anyroad. Well Mr Mash weren't willing to get rid of her, he makes her housekeeper and that's the position her held right up to her sad demise. On 8 December it were.

'Well Kate, rather Miss Dungey, she come from farming stock, her father had a farm up Abingdon way I think it were. Well it don't matter, but what I'm trying to say is her was used to roughing it a bit. It were a cold old place Lambridge Farm you see and she were up there alone mostly. I was there in the daytime like, with the few men and boys that worked on the farm and in the stables, but it were a lonely place like. Mr Mash would call from time to time and earlier that year his eldest daughter, young Clare, her stayed for a week to keep Miss Dungey company, but going back a year or two, 1891 I think it were, what with that freezing winter, she come down to stay with the Mashes at New Street and I runned the place. Stayed there I did, weren't no hardship. Youm can see the house from my cottage and the missus, she were running across and doing hot meals all day. I never went without I assure you, sir.

'Thank you, sir, much appreciated I'm sure. Where was I now, yes well as I said, Lambridge Wood House was Mash's summer house. That winter 1893 being fairly mild Miss Dungey was up there alone, or she should have been that is, but Mash employed a carpenter, well general dogsbody really, man named Froomes. John Froomes had a wealth of kids ya know, half a dozen of the bleeders, and 'im having a cottage just crosst the road from mine and not a square foot bigger, they was a bit crowded like so John had this agreement like that two of his boys slept up the big house to keep Miss Dungey company. Them boys, James were the older one of 'bout thirteen or fourteen, can't remember the second one's name tho', so 'elp me. Well them boys used to do a few odd jobs round the farm at lunchtime and then back up to the house about 5 and stay the night. Mr Mash never knowed, not that he'd have cared much iffen he had.

'Well 8 December, let me see, I'd just chucked me job in two days previous, but that's a different matter. Well 8 December them two boys reckoned they see Walter Rathall as they come home about 1 o'clock acting suspicious like, but we'll leave that as may be. At 4.30 in the afternoon a farmer that lived some half a mile up the road heard this scream, said it lasted some seven or eight seconds. Came from the direction of Lambridge he said. I remember thinking to meself at the time, seven or eight seconds, that's a fair old scream. [Lillywhite was later to depose in court that he knew what the time was because he'd just heard the 4.30 knocking-off siren at Frouds Wood Mill.] Anyway nobody thought nothing of it at the time.

'At 5.30 James Froomes and his brother went up the big house for supper and bed, but the place was in darkness. They couldn't make no one hear so I suppose they played around a while like kids do, and then went back [they said in court that they waited till about 10 o'clock and then come down for their father]. They were in a hell of a state according to John, specially the little 'un. I think they had got 'emselves in a state telling stories. Well John Froomes was a bit worried see, so he and 'is son James came over for me. I pointed out like that I didn't work for Mr Mash no

The tranquil Thames at Henley; the little town was to erupt with murder fever in 1893

more, but he asked me to come anyroad. Well I put on me boots and I fetches me bullseye lamp and the three of us jaled up to the farm to see what were amiss.

'First thing we discovered was the bay window was half open. When we gets in through the window we found blood on the handle and blood in the room and a poker laying half acrosst the carpet. "Touch nothin'," I sez to John, "this be a matter for the police." Well we gets out and we're going for the law like, when we come across Miss Dungey's body, it were beaten like a bit of raw meat, terrible to behold and alongside her lay this potato masher as they called it, bloody great Indian club it were, 3 or 4 feet long with a girt swollen head on it. Well I waited by the body while John Froomes and his boy went for the law. It weren't no joke standing there I can tell yer. Well finally they come, dozens of 'em with a medical man, Dr George Smith. They touched nothin' till morning, just guarded the body like. Well in the morning they took a statement off me and that was all I wanted to know on the subject.

'Thank you, sir, more than generous I'm sure. Rathall you ask, Walter Rathall to be sure. Well Walter was down on his luck which weren't nothing unusual, he ain't been working at the time, not that he ain't been trying, but there weren't nothing about. Well him and his missus and his young chavey was lodging with Josh and Emily Ayres at The Red Lion at Well Street, grog shop it were, beerhouse and doss house more like, they were kipped up there three to a bed in some cases.

'On 8 December apparently Walter had gone out about 9 o'clock in the morning. Mind you I'm only going on the evidence Emily Ayres gave the court at a later date. She said Walter returned between 10 and 11 and played with his baby for a while. He told his wife he had been beating for Mr McKenzie at Fawley and would be paid that evening. This of course pleased both Mrs Ayres and Mrs Rathall, one being short of the rent like and the other being short of food. According to Emily Ayres, Walter went out again at 4.30 and came back home between 7.15 and 7.30. Once again he had no money. He explained that the foreman could not change a £5 cheque and that he would be paid in the morning. Mrs Rathall reluctantly accepted this.

'On 9 December Rathall went out early and returned at midday. In the meantime like, the police had come looking for him on account of the Froomes brothers saying they had see'd him about the farm of late on a number of occasions. I'd also seen him there and I told police so. When he come in the door at midday, still with no money incidentally, Emily ups and sez to him, "Walter, the police have been here lookin' for you. They think you was involved in that young woman's murder. Now you tell me the truth if you was." Walter turns and he looks at Emily Ayres like and he says, "Believe me Emily, I would not touch a hair of that lovely young woman's head." With this he turns and goes up to his room.

'It were two days later and Walter still ain't heard nothing. It were like he was expecting a tap on the shoulder any time. Well then Walter done a silly thing see, he went and lit out, grabbed his wife and baby like, and took to the hills. Well that done it, them that had suspected him before, well them was sure now, don't get no innocent men running away do 'ee.

'Have 'ee got another drop there, sir, this is a dry old tale. Thank 'ee kindly. Well Superintendent Francis Keal of Oxford was in charge of the case and iffen he'd had any doubts about Walter's guilt before, well 'ee certainly didn't have now. He sent a description of Walter Rathall all over the country and if that weren't enough Mr Mash offered a £100 reward.

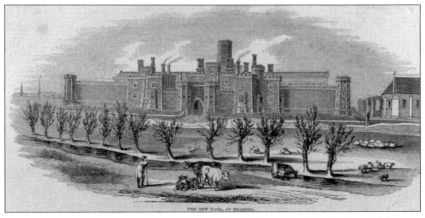

Early (above) and more recent (below) views of Reading Gaol, where Walter
Rathall was lodged awaiting the inquest at Henley

'Walter, he give 'em a fair old run for their money, laying up by day and travelling by night. Well I told 'em he'd head for 'ereford, I thought well £100 wouldn't go amiss would it. It seems however they got him at Daventry. About three weeks he'd been on the run when Inspector Webster came across him in a workhouse. "Is your name Rathall?" enquired Webster. "My name is Tom Brown. If you don't believe me ask my wife," replied Walter, pointing to his missus.

'"His name is Walter Rathall," stated his wife, who was obviously disillusioned with the whole affair. Webster took him straight up to the local lock-up and contacted Superintendent Keal.

'Walter Rathall was well known in Henley, and the story had spread all over the papers, him being on the run all them weeks and so on. He was lodged in Reading Gaol when they got him back, and because it were such a heinous crime there were a lot of locals that didn't mean to do him no good. They was lined along the streets the day of his initial appearance, that must have been 5 January. Henley court was surrounded, but Keal was a clever sod, he smuggled him in among a load of coppers dressed in a policeman's cape. He were only in court a couple of minutes, come up before Colonel Makins he did, just charged like and then remanded till 11 January.

'It were on 12 January when he actually did appear for what they call a magisterial inquiry. You'd never seen so many magistrates in all your born days, or so many police, Walter was shuffled in between ten of 'em. Mr Wilson was chairman, Mr Simmonds and Mr Vandstegen, Mr Ovey and Mr Raikes was there, every local hierarchy and landowner for miles around. Mr Brain were for the prosecution and Mr Woods for the defence.

'Well I won't bore you with repeating all the evidence, but Mr and Mrs Mash and their daughter all gave evidence, also Lillywhite and the Froomes, and I was called to give account of the finding of the body. At mid-morning Dr George Smith took the stand and he described how Miss Dungey's face was covered in dirt, there were fifteen lacerations to her head, there were a 6 inch wound in her neck with what he called a severed jugular. Her torso were badly bruised and he stated that she had one helluva pasting, that blows had been delivered with exhibits A and B (the poker and the masher), then went on to say that there had also been a sharp instrument, probably a knife, which the police had as yet been unable to identify. Dr Smith said that the victim had been deceased between twelve and eighteen hours when he did his tests on it at 10 o'clock on the morning of 9 December.

'The worst evidence for Walter come from Mrs Emily Ayres, you know, her saying he were out about the time when the deed was done, but Mr Woods gave her a fair old roasting in cross-examination. "How many people were lodging at The Red Lion on the 8th?" asked Mr Woods. "Some six or seven as far as I can recollect", says Emily. "Let me assure you, Mrs Ayres, you had eight. Six men and two women and I have not mentioned the children." Emily Ayres reddened like. "Can you tell me the names of these people?" enquired Mr Woods. Emily remembered five or six names and Mr Woods reminded her of the other two. Then he turned to Emily and fired about five or six names at her asking at what times they came and went during 8 December. Poor old Emily, she's had it. She can't remember when they've come and gone. "And yet you presume to tell the court at what time Walter Rathall came and went. Is it not possible that he may have come and gone several times without you noticing him?" says Woods. "It is unlikely", says Emily, shaken like. "Isn't it also possible that Walter Rathall had been in bed all afternoon without you knowing?" "It's not likely", replied Emily. "Is it possible?" shouts Woods. "Yes, it is", says Emily. "Thank you, no more questions", says Mr Woods.

'Later a Mr Thomas Good was called. He was head gamekeeper for Mr McKenzie at Fawley. Mr Brain asks him one question. "Had Walter Rathall been employed as a beater on 8 December?" "No, sir", said Good. "When was Rathall last employed as a beater?" asks Mr Brain. "Not for over a year", says Good. "No more questions", says Mr Brain. Defence declined questioning Good.

'Inspector Webster of Daventry then give his evidence about the arrest of Walter and how he had tried to give a false name, also he showed a pair of boots he'd taken off the prisoner at the time of arrest. Later Superintendent Keal gave a lot of testimony, most of it circumstantial if I be any judge, but then he comes to the boots and he says these are the same boots whose footprints match the marks left outside the bay window at Lambridge Farm. At this there was a lot of toing and froing between counsels concerning whether this evidence was admissible or not.

'Mr Woods pointed out that there were dozens of pairs of similar boots worn by working men all over the country and if they were Rathall's he'd walked to Daventry at least since then. Not only that, police officers and witnesses had trudged all over the garden on the day of 9 December. In the end like, Mr Wilson decided it was not admissible. Bit reluctant tho', I thought.

'Well later on Walter takes the stand. He's a good-looking cove with a ready wit. There were all sorts of mundane questions, but the nitty gritty seemed to be down to this. Why had he lied to his wife and Mrs Ayres about where he'd been that day? Simple he says, he didn't want his wife to know he had no money, nor no likelihood of none. The same thing applied to Emily Ayres. If her had known what situation he was in she'd have kicked him and his family out.

'Why had he taken off just after the murder? He hadn't, he'd waited nearly three days in case the police called again, but they hadn't. Then as he'd said earlier, there wasn't no work about so he'd set off for 'ereford to try and find some. Why had he avoided the police and lied to Inspector

Miss Blandy in her cell in Oxford Castle.
(From an unpublished Sepia Drawing in the Collection of Mr. Horace Bleackley.)

Henley had not experienced a murder since Mary Blandy was hanged for poisoning her father in 1752. (Photograph by courtesy of Berkshire County Library)

Webster? He couldn't read nor write and as he went about the country he heard people talking like he'd already been convicted, this scared him, so he'd kept to the hills. There were no more questions from either side when I was suddenly recalled as a witness.

'Thank you, sir, perhaps one for the road and a little drop of rum, fine. 'Tis taters out there by the looks. Well I was surprised when I was recalled. They reminded me I was still on oath and Mr Woods says to me, "Mr Dawson, was one of your duties for Mr Mash to transport him about in his dog cart and coach to and from Lambridge?" "Yes", says I. "Who was in residence on such an occasion?" "Why Miss Dungey", I replies. The court was hushed, they all knew where the questions was leading. "Was Miss Dungey alone?" asks Mr Woods. "To the best of my knowledge she were", says I. I didn't owe Mr Mash no 'legiance now, no longer working for him see. "To the best of your knowledge", says Mr Woods, "would Mr Mash have any way of getting home?" "No", says I. "Objection", shouts Mr Brain. I could tell all the magistrates was getting upset, Mr Mash was as red as a beetroot. "Overruled", shouts Mr Wilson most embarrassed. Mr Woods kept it up like and Mr Mash was livid. "Mr Dawson," says he, "did you ever have occasion to drive Mr Mash down to Redcliffe Gardens at New Street?" "Many times," I says; "I'd pick him up from the London train at the station and take him there." "Was Miss Dungey ever in residence there alone?" "Several times", says I.

'By now there was a sort of merriment going round the court. Sort of like the crowd was spurring me on. Mr Brain stood up. "I cannot see the point of this line of questioning," says he. There were uproar, serve 'em right, overpowering holier-than-thou stuffed shirts.

'Mr Woods continued, "Mr Dawson," he says, the crowd quiet now and wondering what's comin next, "can you remember any violent ortication between Mrs Mash and Miss Dungey?" "Ortication, sir?" says I. "Yes, Mr Dawson, you know, a violent disagreement, a to-do." "Why yes," I said. "I remember one ortication in particular, sir, when Mrs Mash was swingin' at Miss Dungey with her umbrella and swearing she'd kill her, sir. With poor Mr Mash trying to get atween 'em, sir." The audience loved this, but the magistrates didn't. I didn't care, it were all gospel truth anyroad. Mr Wilson however, he'd had enough. "Mr Woods," he says, "can you explain to me how in any way this line of questioning is pertaining to the accusation made against your client?" "Your Honour," says Mr Woods, "since I have been in this court I have not heard one word of evidence that is pertaining to the accusation made against my client." "That is another matter," shouted Mr Wilson, but it were all over by then, there was a bit of summing up, but Mr Wilson was a fair man. Walter Rathall, with the eloquence of Mr Woods, had won the day. The jury brought a verdict of insufficient evidence to go to trial.

'Walter, well Walter were a popular man then. Them that had come to abuse him carried him out shoulder-high and that were the end on it.

'Right you are then, sir, just the one coz Jake be closing now. Nope, nobody were charged, well they hasn't been as yet as far as I knows. That rum fair gone to my head, sir.

'Who done her? I don't know who done her, 'twern't Walter, leastways I don't think so. He were wicked like, dishonest, weak, a bugger for the women, but I ain't never knowed him violent.

'Old man Mash, I don't know, she might have become an embarrassment but he had money. He'd a got some other poor sod to do it for a few quid. Same applies to the old girl, she didn't like Kate for obvious reasons, and the daughter Clare, maybe she see'd her parents drifting apart, but it's a bit far-fetched, her wouldn't have known where to find no assassin.

'Nope, it were probably what the law calls an opportune crime. Kate might have surprised some itinerant tramp during a burglary, you know, she'd have gone for him with the poker, he might of grabbed it and given her a pasting then dragged her outside and give her another one with the old tater-masher. Never did find no knife, but he could have took that with him. The varieties is endless. People have put forward many, what's the word? Sinarios. Don't s'pose no one will ever know.

'Anyway good night, sir, thanks for the drinks. I will tell yer one thing before I goes. Little Miss Perfect Dungey, she weren't so lily-white and innocent, she'd been around. Old Mash and her was intimate, that's for sure, and paying highly for the privilege I'll be bound, and if rumour is to be believed so was the brother-in-law. Handsome, useless, work-shy Walter, God's gift to bleeding women, but what about poor old George? He tried it on a couple of times and she went dinnello. Hollered and shouted, called me names, I was only horsin' around like. Never meant no harm but she reared up fit to be tied, said she'd tell my missus, the bitch. Well she didn't but she told old Mash and he asked me to hand me job in. Sort of offer I couldn't refuse you know. Spiteful bitch lost me the best job I ever had. I ain't done no good since. Women like that needs bustin' and breakin' to pieces, they deserves all they gets, that's what I says.

'Well, good night, sir, I nearly lost me rag then, terrible temper I got, so the missus says. Less said soonest mended that's my motto. Thanks again, sir.'

CHAPTER EIGHT

GEORGE BARKER, A BLACKSMITH OF WOKINGHAM, ACCUSED OF MURDERING HIS BROTHER

On 6 June 1911 at Reading, George Barker was indicted for feloniously killing his brother Henry. For the defence was Mr Ralph Thomas, for the prosecution was the popular and prominent Mr Sturgess. The facts were not in doubt but the interpretation of them was.

The brothers had inherited the family blacksmith business from their deceased father several years previously. They had also inherited their mother Ann Barker. Should there be any discord in the running of the family business, any stalemate in decision-making, then the mother acted as a matriarchal arbitrator and cast the deciding vote. A duty, it must be said, she was rarely requested to perform. As the main criterion of small businesses is to show a profit, those whose fortune it is to share in that profit rarely disagree to any major extent. There may be, however, slightly varying ideas of how to obtain the common goal. Such the was case with the Barker brothers.

On the surface the small workforce (the brothers, one regular man, one part-time man and a bellows boy) worked and spoke in harmony. George and Henry were genuinely fond of each other and were liked and respected by their small staff.

The smithy, with cottage combined, in Station Road, Wokingham, was popular both with local tradespeople and the local aristocracy. Horse-shoeing was obviously the establishment's mainstay but the brothers were receiving more and more work from local farmers, repairing their machinery.

Flourishing trade was inevitably coupled with increasing credit and it was on this point that the brothers held widely differing opinions. An over-simplistic view of the situation was that George favoured the tried and

Reading, where George Barker was indicted for the felonious killing of his brother Henry. (Photograph by courtesy of Berkshire Books and Prints)

trusted way of doing things, cash on the nail as soon as the job was finished. Henry took the more enlightened outlook that you could not expect a farmer or any other business man to dip in his pocket straightaway after having his plough repaired; invoices and statements were the correct procedure.

Henry ran the accounts, but in George's view with far too much flexibility. The chronological course of events is best described in the evidence given by Charles White in court. White was the brothers' sole full-time employee and the only man on duty that fateful morning of 2 May.

Charles White deposed that the brothers had both been good-humoured that morning and all three men had worked with a will. At 11 a.m. George had gone next door to The Hope and Anchor to bring back beer for the men's refreshment. As they drank, still in good humour, George casually enquired of his brother if a certain customer had paid his account that morning as he had promised. Henry replied that he had not, but he would probably be dropping it in later.

George remarked that they could not pay their suppliers and feed their families on probabilities, he was going to call for the money as soon as he'd finished his ale. Henry remonstrated with his brother, saying that George had lost them several good customers by rudely demanding money.

The argument quickly grew into a heated row. Then as George went to head for the back door, Henry, obviously fearing he was going to demand money from the respected customer, attempted to bar his way. The upshot was that the brothers wrestled and tripped through the back door and into the yard.

As both brothers were younger, bigger and stronger than he, White returned to his work. They were his employers and he considered that it was not his affair. Mrs Ann Barker was still emotionally affected as she described the events of the afternoon of 2 May. She related that she had discovered her son Henry lying in the yard; he complained of terrible pain in his leg and was shaking uncontrollably. She had summoned help to transport him into the house, where his condition had rapidly deteriorated. Dr Bokenham was called and he also alerted PC Burke. The doctor had in

In 1911 the quiet town of Wokingham was agog with the news of the death of a local blacksmith

turn called for aid to rush Henry to the Royal Berkshire Hospital but unfortunately Henry died during the journey.

Dr Bokenham deposed that Henry Barker had sustained a broken leg and was suffering from delirium tremens. In answer to a question from Mr Ralph Thomas the doctor stated that one could not suffer delirium tremens unless one had consumed quantities of alcohol over substantial periods of time.

Joseph Maurice Capon, landlord of The Hope and Anchor, informed the court that he had heard a deluge of foul language and heated argument coming from next door. He had peered over the fence and had seen Henry Barker lying on the ground with George Barker walking away. They were some 7 feet from the back door near a manure heap.

Mr Sturgess was on his feet. He turned to the publican, 'Surely,' he said, 'in your statement to PC Burke you stated that you heard noises as if somebody were being kicked and when you looked over the fence you saw

The Hope and Anchor, Wokingham, showing on the left the entrance to the Barkers' business

George Barker in an aggressive attitude, with his fists clenched, leaning over the body of his brother.' 'I may have said so at the time,' Capon replied, 'but on reflection I realize I may have been mistaken.' Joseph Capon regained his seat, his credibility a little suspect.

Things were looking good for George Barker. Dr William S. Whyman, casualty doctor at the Royal Berkshire Hospital, took the stand. He stated that Henry Barker had been dead on his arrival at hospital. X-rays had revealed a double fracture of the left leg. Delirium tremens had been brought about by a sudden shock to the system, and this in turn had caused heart failure which had been responsible for the unfortunate man's demise.

In answer to a question Dr Whyman pronounced that it was possible, but unlikely, that a person could experience delirium tremens without excessive alcohol being present in the system. He was, however, quite prepared to believe that this could be the case concerning Henry Barker.

Dr Whyman continued that he had carefully studied the body and found no external bruising whatsoever, there was nothing at all conducive with a kick or a punch. At this point Mr Sturgess virtually conceded the case. The bench requested the two lawyers to approach. His esteemed honour instructed the jury that there was no case to answer and that they should pronounce a verdict of not guilty. This they duly did and a relieved but saddened George Barker walked to freedom.

CHAPTER NINE

THE MURDER OF SARAH AND ISABELLA ROSE AT LOVE LANE, SHAW, IN OCTOBER 1918

Sarah Rose was an attractive gypsy woman of nineteen. She lived with her family (both close and distant relatives) under canvas at the tiny village of Enborne, some 3 miles to the west of Newbury. Sarah had a daughter, six-month-old Isabella, offspring of an association with her cousin Joseph Rose.

As with all travelling children Isabella was cared for by the whole of the family. This numbered from fifteen to twenty near relatives and some hundred or more related through marriage or blood, or both.

Gypsy names were generally adopted at will. In fact up until the 1950s, when many true gypsies married wandering Irish tinkers, there were less than two dozen genuine Romany surnames in the whole of southern England.

Sarah's cousin Joseph had not stayed with the family when they moved to Kent for the hop-picking. He had other business down near Bath. He joined them, however, for Newbury Fair on 17 October. The two young people had shared the same tent since that date.

It was on the morning of 1 October that Joseph and Sarah set out with tiny Isabella for Newbury Market. Joseph needed a wheel and hoped to purchase one there. They were said to be in good spirits and joking with each other as they pushed little Isabella's perambulator along the unmade road from the camp-site to the town.

Love Lane leads between Shaw and Donnington, two villages to the north of Newbury. At 1.20 p.m. on 18 October William Hiscock rode his bicycle along Love Lane and noticed the little trio of gypsy folk on the way to Donnington. The pair of adult gypsies were in a field. They were eating something and seemed to be pushing each other.

Newbury, the town in which Sarah and Isabella Rose were to spend their last morning on earth

At 1.40 Mrs Ada Edge was returning to her village of Shaw from Donnington. All of a sudden a man appeared through a gate in the lane. He made a horrendous sight, his clothes were virtually drenched in blood. He was holding a piece of cloth to a gaping throat wound. Mrs Edge was petrified to the spot, the man's wounds had obviously deprived him of the power of speech which added an uncanny aspect to an already appallingly bizarre situation. The man pointed through the gate from whence he came and tried to pull the terrified woman towards him. It was obvious that he wanted to show her something. Mrs Edge glanced through the gateway and saw two inert bundles which later proved to be the bodies of Sarah and Isabella Rose.

Frederick Schelling, a Swiss baker, was driving his horse-drawn delivery van in Love Lane, Shaw, when he was approached by a very distraught woman and a man who was bleeding profusely from a throat wound. Sending the woman for assistance, the baker followed the gesticulating man into the field. The man was crying and led Mr Schelling to the bodies of a young woman and a very young child. Both had been savagely slain and were covered in blood; their throats had been cut. Joseph Rose pulled

The lofty romantic ruins of
Donnington Castle silently witnessed
the ferocious murders of a young
mother and her infant daughter

the baker away from the bodies, excitedly pointing to a gap in the hedge on
the opposite side of the small field. The gypsy seemed to be indicating that
someone had gone through the cleft in the bushes. Schelling ran quickly to
the gap but could see nobody. He returned to the distraught man and tried
to make him sit down as Rose's panic was obviously aggravating the
bleeding. Having partially accomplished this task he returned to the bodies.
He placed his hand on each; both were warm and had met their demise very
recently. Leaving the scene for a few moments Schelling dashed into the
lane where he stopped a local milk-churn boy, Henry Holloway, and sent
him for medical assistance.

Dr Edmund Hemsted arrived at Love Lane about 2.15. He made a brief
examination of the bodies before placing Rose in his car and rushing him to
Newbury Hospital. Once there he performed an emergency tracheotomy
beneath the wound. The doctor felt tolerably confident that he had saved
the young gypsy's life.

The ensuing inquest was held at Donnington Parish Hall before Coroner

Pinegar. John Rose, father of the deceased and uncle to Joseph Rose, identified the bodies of his daughter Sarah and his granddaughter Isabella. He also stated that Joseph and Sarah were living as man and wife and were on the best of terms. In answer to a question from Mr Pinegar he stated that he had never seen Rose with a knife other than when they were making clothes-pegs.

Superintendent Gamble, in charge of the case, described the position of the bodies and pointed out that they were near the stables of Shaw House. Evidence was then taken from the various witnesses that had been at the scene before and after the tragic events.

A brief letter was read from Joseph Rose, still in a critical condition at

It was near the stables of Shaw House that the bodies of the young gypsy woman and her baby were discovered

Newbury Hospital. The letter stated that he had sat down with his family to eat in the field. A man had appeared from the bushes and attacked all three of them with a knife before fleeing through the gap in the hedge. His wife had recognized the man because she had shouted, 'No Harry, no', as he had committed his murderous assault.

Dr Hemsted took the stand for over an hour. His evidence was thorough and concise. After an exhaustive description of the wounds the doctor informed the court that he was of the opinion that the bodies had been dragged between 2 and 3 yards. When asked if it were possible that Sarah Rose's wounds had been self-inflicted he replied, 'Certainly not.' In answer to another question Hemsted informed the court that Rose had no abrasions to his arms and hands but had sustained no fewer than four minor injuries to the throat, these being tiny in comparison with the one that had all but cost him his life.

At this point Coroner Pinegar thought it impossible to continue without Joseph Rose being present. He adjourned the hearing until 27 November.

On 27 November the inquest was once again adjourned. Rose, having finally recovered from his near fatal wound to the throat, was once again at death's door; he had contracted influenza while in hospital.

Joseph Rose appeared before Mr E. Martin-Aikens at Newbury county police court on 12 December 1918. He was finally adjudged fit enough to plead. He faced three charges: the murder of his wife, the murder of his daughter, and attempted suicide. Rose pleaded not guilty to all three counts. He was remanded to Reading Assizes.

Mr Justice Rowlatt presided over the assizes on 16 January 1919. The prosecution under Mr Lort-Williams MP had decided to proceed initially with one indictment, the murder of Sarah Rose.

Rose's defence counsel was the able Hon. H. Coventry, assisted by the Newbury solicitor Mr C. Lucas. Mr Coventry had decided with Rose that it would probably be beneficial to his case if he did not give direct evidence. During the proceedings Rose did not take the stand, thereby absolving himself from prosecution questions. Proceedings opened with Henry Bell, a Newbury architect who had made a plan to scale of the lanes and fields in the vicinity of the murders.

Mr John Rose was again called and once more endorsed his previous opinion that Joseph Rose and his daughter were on the best of terms at the time of the tragedy. The prosecution was trying to establish a chronological representation of events on an hour-by-hour basis. Mr Lort-Williams then called Mrs Dalsey Black of Newbury. She turned out to be a very controversial witness. Her testimony was extremely damaging for Joseph Rose.

Mrs Black deposed that she had been in Newbury Market at 11.30 a.m. on 28 October when she had noticed the defendant with a young woman and a baby in a perambulator. There had been a harsh verbal exchange of very foul language between the two, and then the defendant had struck the woman in the mouth twice, causing her to stagger.

This evidence was detrimental indeed to Joseph Rose's case. Later in the trial, however, Dr Hemsted was to state that he had found no bruising whatsoever on the face of Sarah Rose.

Evidence pertaining to the discovery of the body and events immediately proceeding the same was provided by William Hiscock, Henry Holloway, Ada Edge and Frederick Schelling. Dr Edmund Hemsted was once again on the stand for several hours; again he provided evidence in an exact and meticulous fashion. The whole court-room was aware that his interpretation of events based on experience and accurate diagnosis could be the deciding factor in the case. His evidence was to be evaluated by the prosecution presently.

PC Richardson, the first police officer on the scene, attested that no weapon had been discovered near the vicinity, but on searching the accused he had found a sharp pocket knife. In answer to a proposition by Mr Coventry the constable agreed that there was no blood on the exhibit.

Superintendent Gamble made his report. The prosecution case was simple: if Rose had not murdered his wife, who had? The time element was very tight and there had been no strangers seen in either Shaw or Donnington that day. There had been a row earlier at Newbury Market and it was obvious by the evidence that it had once again erupted in the afternoon. Rose had murdered his wife and daughter, then tried either to commit suicide or to fake an attack.

Mr Coventry on the other hand could not see how the prosecution came to its misguided point of view. Where was the motive? Joseph and Sarah were on the best of terms, Mr Coventry continued; he advised the jury that although no stranger had been noticed in either village, there had been any number of itinerants passing through Newbury, only 2 miles to the south. Market day attracted any amount of unknown quantities. Also the jury should take little or no notice of Mrs Black's testimony, the lady was not 100 per cent sure that this was the same couple that were involved in the earlier fracas, and in fact Dr Hemsted's evidence later proved that there had been no such attack on Sarah Rose.

If Mr Coventry was to quote Dr Hemsted on this occasion in hope of an acquittal, then he would have to accept that other evidence from the same source argued strongly for conviction. There were two undeniable facts that would seem to disprove that any other entity (i.e. 'Harry') was involved in the equation.

One irrefutable fact was that there were no abrasions on Rose's hands. Another was there were four small abrasions on Rose's throat, other than the deep and nearly fatal one. Surely if a man were to see his wife and six-month-old child attacked with a knife he would make some sort of move in their defence, thereby sustaining some type of injury to his hands or arms. In the extreme unlikelihood of his not showing any form of bravery or endeavour to save them, then surely he would make some kind of preventive gesture to save his own miserable life. It is a natural reflex to put one's arms up in self-defence. But Rose had no injury whatsoever either to hand, wrist or forearm.

He did, however, have four very minor wounds to his throat. Dr Hemsted described them as trial runs, and on the face of it, what else could they be? A man attempting to cut his own throat, either to the extreme of self-inflicted termination, or to such an extent that one would surmise that that had been his intention, would certainly have a couple of practice runs. There could be no other cause or reason for such wounds.

The jury didn't think so anyway, it took them less than five minutes' deliberation to find Joseph Rose guilty. Mr Justice Rowlatt sentenced the young gypsy to death without a tremor of emotion.

Mr Coventry launched an appeal on 3 February 1919. Rose now stated that he wished to give evidence and claimed that he was not given sufficient opportunity at the trial. Mr Justice Bray refused to make the concession. Joseph Rose, aged twenty-five, was hanged at Oxford a fortnight later.

Whereas there can be no doubt that Rose murdered his wife and daughter, one can never be entirely certain as to whether or not he intended to take his own life. If it was a charade to reinforce his story about 'Harry' then it was an extremely hazardous one. He was only snatched from the jaws of death by the medical efficiency and expedience of Dr Hemsted.

CHAPTER TEN

THE MURDER OF SARAH BLAKE, LANDLADY OF THE CROWN AND ANCHOR AT GALLOWS TREE COMMON, BY JACK HEWETT

In 1922 The Crown and Anchor was a somewhat remote inn in a tiny hamlet, beside a back road from Pangbourne to Henley. The hamlet that rejoiced in the somewhat intimidating name of Gallows Tree Common was a mere smattering of houses in which every inhabitant either knew or was related to his neighbour.

The ancient inn was controlled and maintained by a widow of fifty-five named Sarah Blake. She was a popular and jovial woman and the archetypal landlady that would brook no nonsense.

At 6.15 p.m. on 3 March 1922 Sarah Blake had a brief conversation with her nearest neighbour, a Mrs Payne; the lady had dropped by on a small errand. She was there only briefly and noticed that the bar was empty except for a local lad, Jack Hewett, a farmer's workboy of fifteen, who was downing a raspberryade at one of the bench tables.

At 7.50 that same evening a farm labourer, Harry Dowling of Kidmore End, was taking his father and brother down to The Crown and Anchor for a pint. On arrival the trio were surprised to find the pub closed and in darkness. After a disappointed oath or two the three men traipsed to The Reformation, a short walk up the road. At 8 p.m. or thereabouts Albert Hewett, the stepfather of Jack Hewett, sent the lad down to The Crown and Anchor to purchase some beer for his consumption at home. The lad was gone for some time; when he returned he stated that The Crown and Anchor was closed and that he had had to walk to The Reformation for the ale. A courting couple were also to state later that they had knocked for a drink and received no reply.

Newspaper cutting of Mrs Sarah Blake

Mrs Payne pushed open the door of The Crown and Anchor at 8.30 the following morning. The sight that met her eyes was appalling. Mrs Blake lay dead in her bar parlour. Her injuries were horrendous; blood was spattered on doors and cupboards and even the ceiling. Sarah Blake had been beaten and stabbed with the ferocity of a madman, and had finally been despatched with a cut throat.

Mrs Payne ran for her husband Alfred and together they went for the police. The police arrived in the shape of PC Buswell of nearby Rotherfield Peppard, who was shortly followed by Dr Gandy who quickly confirmed the suspicion that Sarah Blake had died of a severed throat. He was also able to tell the police the time of death, between 6 p.m. and 8 p.m. the previous evening, and that the unfortunate woman had been stabbed many times with a knife that had a broken point.

The famous Dr Spilsbury, brought down from London, was later to state at the inquest that the body contained over sixty stab wounds and also that the skull was fractured in four places. The throat was cut from the left ear to the spinal cord. Both a stabbing instrument and a bludgeon implement must have been applied in this ferocious attack.

Within a matter of hours an army of police officers had descended on the tiny community, their main purpose being to find the murder weapons. After several days with teams of officers combing the ground on their knees, neither implement had come to light. Certain other exhibits had, however. The front door key was found by PC Russel, already rusting. PC Grant found a bucket of discoloured water in the pub yard; this, however, was poured away – the first of several police blunders. The officer described it as a light brown colour consistent with blood. Later at the Oxford Assizes a wily lawyer was to suggest to Grant that it could also be consistent with the discolouration caused by ale glasses being washed in it. The officer grudgingly admitted that this could very well be the case.

It was at this stage, after several days of enquiry had got absolutely nowhere, that Scotland Yard was brought in. Superintendent Wastie, Inspector Heldon and Sergeant Ryan set up headquarters at Caversham police station. The case was now five days old and the trail was rapidly going cold.

On 9 March a PC Hudson noticed young Jack Hewett staring into the hedgerow near the inn. The young constable thought little of it but made a mental note as the same hedgerow had been combed by a dozen officers on two previous occasions. It was, however, within hours that the police got what would seem to have been their first breakthrough. Superintendent Wastie was called from the scene of the crime by an officer with an urgent message, 'Can you come to Caversham at once, sir? A man has confessed to Sarah Blake's murder.'

Frederick Alfred Sheppard was a labourer by excuse, and a burglar by inclination. He lived with his widowed mother at 65 Rupert Street, Reading. He had been arrested earlier that week for a break-in at Victoria Square, Reading. He had approached the constable on duty the second night of his incarceration and had admitted to being one of two men involved in the widow's murder. Sheppard now wanted some sort of deal involving the dropping of the Victoria Square case for information on The Crown and Anchor atrocity.

Superintendent Wastie heard the man out. Several items of information about the Sarah Blake case had been kept from the newspapers so as not to

Newspaper cutting of Frederick
Alfred Sheppard

jeopardize the enquiries. Sheppard stated that on 3 March he had been
drinking late in Henley. Being broke he had decided to walk back to Reading,
a direct distance of about 8 miles (Gallows Common is some 3 miles off the
direct route). On his way Sheppard had struck up an acquaintance with a man
named Jack Larkins, a fellow pedestrian who was also down on his luck. As
they reached The Crown and Anchor, Jack suggested that they break in.
Sheppard had wanted nothing to do with this idea but had grudgingly
accepted the role of look-out. Larkins had entered the pub through an upstairs
window. There was a scream followed by the sound of a struggle and the
noise of somebody being struck repeatedly. A few minutes later Larkins had
reappeared covered in blood. This had terrified Sheppard who then decided
to drop Larkins' acquaintance as soon as possible.

Superintendent Wastie listened with interest. 'Are you telling me the
whole truth?' he asked the prisoner. 'And about what time did you and
Larkins arrive at the inn?' 'About 4 a.m. sir,' Sheppard answered.

Superintendent Wastie looked Sheppard straight in the eye. 'You are a lying hound,' he said. 'Don't waste my time.' Wastie knew that Sheppard had had nothing to do with the murder; first there was the time discrepancy and second there had been no evidence of a burglary. For reasons best known to themselves, possibly while they tried to trace the elusive Larkins, possibly because they had no other suspect, and probably out of spite, the police remanded Sheppard in custody until 4 April. He was finally released on 5 May when all charges against him were dropped.

It was also in mid-March that PC Rippington discovered a knife under the hedgerow near The Crown and Anchor. As stated before, this hedge had already been thoroughly searched on two occasions by a dozen or more officers. The knife had been purposely hidden under leaves and, as Dr Gandy had predicted, had lost its point. It also had dried blood on it and several hairs attached to it.

This was a breakthrough indeed. The news also nudged the memory of PC Hudson. He went straight to Inspector Heldon and informed him that he had seen Jack Hewett staring at that very spot. The knife was forwarded to the famous Home Office analyst John Webster. Sergeant Ryan was then dispatched to Jack Hewett's house and returned with a brown-stained tunic. This was also forwarded to Webster along with a door-knocker, some blood-soaked sheets of paper and Sarah Blake's woollen shawl. Webster returned all the items stating that he could identify Mrs Blake's blood on all

The knife which was found in the hedge near The Crown and Anchor Inn, Gallows Tree Common, and which the boy Hewitt has said was his.

The knife used in the Crown and Anchor case

the other samples, but was unsure of the stains on the tunic. They were definitely bloodstains, but he could not be sure if they belonged to Mrs Blake, or how old the stains were.

PC Buswell's next step was to take the knife to Jack Hewett to enquire about the ownership. The boy denied all knowledge of the knife and his stepfather stated categorically that he had never seen it among the boy's possessions. PC Buswell then played his hunch; he took the knife to Joseph Haynes, a young acquaintance of Hewett. Haynes was just as emphatic that the knife did belong to Hewett, he had seen him with it many times and had even borrowed it on several occasions.

Armed with this evidence PC Buswell approached Superintendent Wastie. On 4 April Wastie in turn, accompanied by Inspector Heldon and Sergeant Ryan, proceeded to Padwicke Farm where Hewett was employed at a princely 12s a week. Hewett was questioned for two hours by the three detectives. He denied that he had been staring over the hedge at the exact spot where the knife was found. He denied ownership of the knife. He also unequivocally refuted Haynes's claim that he had loaned him a knife and vehemently contradicted the inference that the blood on his tunic belonged to Mrs Blake. Hewett stated that he regularly killed chickens and rabbits on the farm and that this was in all probability the source of such stains.

The detectives did not like the answer. Hewett was arrested and taken to Caversham police station where he was charged with the murder of Sarah Blake. It was at Caversham that Hewett first admitted the crime.

Jack Hewett asked PC Buswell if he could see his newspaper. He then pointed to a picture of the interior of The Crown and Anchor. 'That's my glass of stout on the table,' he said. The young constable saw his opening; he encouraged Hewett to say more.

The farmboy elaborated at length. PC Buswell decided to take it down in the form of a statement. Hewett had called to see Mrs Blake, not an unusual event. With her permission he had poured himself first a raspberry champagne and then a glass of ginger stout. At 6 p.m. a customer, Alf Payne, came in and then left, shortly after this his wife visited for a few minutes. When Hewett and Mrs Blake were again alone he picked up a metal bar that was used to help shift the barrels and struck her over the head with it several times. Jack Hewett stated that he had no idea why he had done it.

Hewett went on to say that he took out his knife and stabbed his victim

THE HENLEY MURDER.

Lonely Inn Where Crime Was Committed.

The South Oxfordshire Coroner opened on Tuesday the inquest on Mrs. Sarah Blake, whose badly battered body was discovered on Saturday in a room at the rear of the bar at the Crown and Anchor Inn, a lonely house at Gallows Tree Common, Henley, of which she was the sole occupant. Evidence given by Dr. Spilsbury showed there were sixty wounds on the body. The inquiry was adjourned for a fortnight.　　[Photo by May.

Mr. and Mrs. Payne, who live next door to the inn. It was Mrs. Payne who first discovered the tragedy.　　[Photo by C. E. May.

SEARCHING FOR CLUES IN THE GARDEN.　　[Photo by C. E. May.

Newspaper cuttings about the Crown and Anchor case

time and time again. He then slit her throat to make sure she was dead. At no time did he have any idea why he was acting in such a fashion, the motive certainly wasn't money. Jack Hewett then washed his hands in a bucket of water in the yard, returned and took 2*d* from the till (which incidentally contained some £3) and then went home. On his way he bought 2*d*'s worth of dates at Mr Smith's, a local grocer.

Smith was contacted and substantiated that Jack Hewett had in fact visited his premises at 6.35 and purchased the dates. Hewett signed the confession; he seemed relieved to have got it off his chest. When asked if he had any notion why he had behaved in such an outrageous manner he simply said, 'Blame it on the pictures' (the cinema). It would seem that Jack was an avid cinema-goer. This was the first case in history where it was suggested that violence on the screen could be in some way responsible for corrupting and affecting an individual's behaviour on the street.

Jack Hewett was bailed to appear at Caversham police court on 5 May, Mr Arthur Septon Cohen appearing for the prosecution, Mr Gush for the

Newspaper cutting of Jack Hewitt

defence. The hearing was tolerably brief, it being a foregone conclusion that this was a matter for the Oxford Assizes. Many witnesses were heard; however, most of the evidence was from police and medical people.

There was a new witness for the prosecution in the comely shape of Miss Eliza Wheeler. Miss Wheeler resided at 29 Gallows Tree Common, very close to The Crown and Anchor. The witness recounted an episode which had taken place some two days before the murder. Wheeler had been in the bar parlour when she heard such phrases as 'Take more care in future, young man' and 'Please remember next time, Jack'. Mr Gush was at once on his feet. 'If there had been a row between Mrs Blake and Jack Hewett only two days previously, why was he in The Crown and Anchor on the fateful night drinking raspberryade? Indeed raspberryade that Mrs Blake had given him. These would hardly seem the actions of two people at loggerheads. Mr Gush then asked Eliza Wheeler if it was not a fact that there had been bad blood between the Hewetts and the Wheelers for some years; the witness denied this emphatically.

It was at this stage that the magistrates decided to adjourn the case to Oxford Assizes, but not before Mr Gush had made it clear to the court that he was far from happy with the way in which Scotland Yard had treated his client. He informed the assembly that his client had made a statement of confession, a confession that he had since withdrawn. 'Was it moral, or even ethical, for three experienced police officers, Heldon, Wastie and Ryan, to question a fifteen-year-old boy for long hours without that boy having any legal representation, and then to take him to Caversham police station where further enquiries were made by PC Buswell? Was it any wonder that a frightened boy would confess to almost anything under these circumstances?' With this the proceedings came to an end.

Jack Hewett was arraigned at Oxford Assizes on 2 June 1922 before Mr Justice Shearman. J.B. Matthews KC and Graham Millward were for the prosecution, Mr E.C. Gates conducted the defence. The court was packed, the witnesses numerous. Harry Dowling and his brother were to describe the inn being closed. They were followed by Alf Payne and his wife whose evidence placed Hewett in the bar at 6.15 p.m. (a fact that the defence had never denied). The Paynes with PC Buswell described the discovery of the body. Forensic and medical evidence was forwarded by such famous names as Dr Spilsbury and Mr John Webster, ably abetted by Dr Gandy.

The ever immaculate and world-famous Sir Bernard Spilsbury, whose involvement brought national interest to the Gallows Tree Common murder. Spilsbury discovered no fewer than sixty stab wounds and four fractures of the skull on the corpse of Sarah Blake

PC Grant, PC Russel, PC Hudson and PC Rippington gave practical evidence concerning the pail of water and the knife. The knife was also identified by Joseph Haynes. The last of the civilian witnesses was Mr J. Smith who kept the tiny shop at Gallows Tree Common; he affirmed that Hewett had indeed spent 2*d* on dates in his shop that evening, thereby confirming part of the much-disputed confession.

Later in the day came evidence from Inspector Heldon, Superintendent Wastie, Sergeant Ryan and once again PC Buswell concerning the confession. This was Mr Gates's chance, he went for the throat. If Gush had previously been critical of police methods, Gates was ruthlessly scathing. Gates began by saying the police had obtained the confession in peculiar circumstances to say the least. He inferred that Hewett had been interrogated rather than questioned by Messrs Heldon, Wastie and Ryan, and that he had been virtually bullied into signing a statement by PC Buswell at Caversham. The confession made an absolute mockery of the word 'voluntary'. We have here a boy of somewhat limited intelligence

Hewett's defenders, Mr Gates and Mr Gush. Mr Gush, on the left, was at 6 ft 6 in the tallest lawyer on the circuit. (Photograph by courtesy of Berkshire Reference Library)

being interrogated by three of Scotland Yard's most experienced officers for several hours and then taken to Caversham where he is placed in the custody of the large and formidable PC Buswell.

When Hewett took the stand he vehemently denied harming Mrs Blake. He had left her at 6.20 in good health. He had returned at 8 p.m. and found the pub in darkness and he knew nothing else. In answer to Mr Matthews KC he stated that he had never owned or seen the knife before, also that he had made the statement at Caversham because he was terrified. In answer to Mr Gates he stated that he was in the toilet for much of the time at Caversham when PC Buswell wrote out the statement. When the officer had given it to him to read and sign there were many words he could not decipher and even more that he couldn't comprehend.

The prosecution's final remarks were based on asking whether this crime could have been committed by anybody other than the defendant. J.B. Matthews thought not. He went on to make much of the knife and the confession. Mr Gates's final address was nothing if not eloquent. 'If one ignores the rightly controversial confession, what is one left with in this case? Virtually nothing,' he answered himself rhetorically. 'We have only the knife – the metal bar has not been found – the knife of which we have had evidence from both Hewett and his father that he never owned such a weapon. The prosecution only has the testimony of the youth Joseph Haynes that the defendant ever owned such a knife. Little enough to convict upon surely?' Mr Gates went on to describe the state of mind of Hewett that day. He had returned without the slightest alteration in his disposition and composure. Would it have been possible for a boy of fifteen to commit this most heinous of crimes and then to return home shortly after, calm and composed and showing no sign of stress? Mr Gates thought not, and he was sure the jury would agree with him.

The jury did not. After hearing a rather lengthy summing-up by his lordship, in which he used phrases like 'a considerable body of direct evidence concerning the boy', they brought in a verdict of guilty. It had only taken them half an hour to discuss the case. Retiring at 2 p.m., they had returned at 2.30 with the unanimous verdict.

Mr Justice Shearman pointed out almost apologetically that the law prevented him from announcing the death penalty for one so young. He sentenced Jack Hewett to be detained during His Majesty's pleasure.

CHAPTER ELEVEN

THE MURDER OF JESSIE STATHAM GOLDUP AT MAIDENHEAD ON 26 APRIL 1929

To the local milkman Alexander Kirby it was a normal hard-working day. It was Saturday 26 April 1929, the day he collected the milk money. Heywood's Park at White Waltham near Maidenhead was part of his round; at 8.15 a.m. he knocked on the door of Percy Goldup's bungalow but there was no reply.

The milkman found this a little unusual. Percy, a one-time grocer aged thirty-six, and his wife Jessie, had been in the community for less than a fortnight, and they were always up and about very early. It was strange that there was no sign of life. Kirby made a mental note to call later on; his commission relied on prompt payment.

Unbeknown to the milkman, the Goldups had been seen earlier that day by a man working locally. Aubrey Irving of Fern Cottage, Furze Platt had been tending the garden of a cottage that backed on to the Goldups'. He was later to testify that at 7.30 that morning the woman had come out to collect some washing and that a man had followed her out and gone to the shed.

At 1.30 during his lunch break Alexander Kirby returned to the bungalow but there was still no sign of life. He called again at 3.30 and then finally at 6.30. It was at this time that he suspected foul play and made it his business to try to see the interior of the dwelling through a gap in the curtains. The milkman was in for a shock; even from his restricted viewpoint he could see partially into the bedroom and the hallway. What appeared to be blood was everywhere.

Kirby's ominous suspicions seemingly justified, he rushed with all speed to the nearest police house, that of PC Frank Fraser of White Waltham. The two men returned. Fraser, following procedure, knocked and called briefly before forcing an entrance through the bedroom window. The scene that greeted the two men was horrific; the bedroom and hall were deluged in blood. Two bodies lay on the neatly made bed. One, a female, had substantial head wounds and had bled profusely from the throat; she was obviously dead. From the second body, a male, there was a slight stirring of life; the man also had a substantial throat wound, but as yet it had not proved fatal. Both bodies were clad in night apparel.

PC Fraser directed Kirby and several neighbours who had appeared, as per habit, from various directions. He sent for an ambulance, a local doctor and his superior officer, Inspector Henry Brown of Maidenhead. The house, except for the bloodstains, was particularly neat and well ordered. While waiting for assistance PC Fraser took stock of the situation. There had been no forced entry other than his own, no robbery and apparently no struggle of any intensity.

In the hall Fraser found a bloodstained hammer, at the bedside he discovered a cut-throat razor with part of the blade missing, and also a suicide note addressed to Mr Goldup's mother. Inspector Brown arrived shortly with several men; Fraser handed him the note. It briefly stated that he could go on no longer, he had come to his end through nobody else but 'Jesse', and that Edie and her husband 'was at the bottom of all this'.

Medical help arrived in the unusual form of a local lady doctor, Winifred Irene Franks, who was working under the name of Dr Doherty. Dr Doherty discovered that Jessie Goldup had sustained a fractured skull, the weapon being proved to be the hammer in the hall. The wound that had killed her, however, was the massive razor slash across the windpipe.

On examining Percy Goldup the doctor found a 5 inch gash across the throat with the missing part of the razor still embedded in the wound. The patient was rushed to hospital, later to be interviewed by Inspector Brown.

Percy Robert James Goldup was charged with the murder of Jessie Statham Goldup at Maidenhead magistrates' court on 28 May 1929. It must have been obvious at this stage that Goldup was not a well man mentally. Doctors were brought in who attested to his state of mind. The case, however, was placed before the Oxford Assizes (Reading being too busy) for a swift conclusion, to be heard on 7 June.

The Goldup case at Oxford was presided over by Mr Justice Shearman. Mr A.J. Long conducted the prosecution, for the defence was Mr A.F. Clements. Goldup pleaded not guilty to murder; he was a distraught man and spent much of the trial in tears.

After the preliminary evidence from Alexander Kirby, Aubrey Irving, PC Frank Fraser, Inspector Henry Brown and Dr Doherty (Winifred Franks), the court tried to delve a little into Goldup's recent past. Mrs Edith Jane Snow, sister to Jessie Goldup and wife of Charles Jesse Snow, was brought to the stand. She stated that she lived in Hill Street, Reading. To questions from Mr Long she informed the court that her sister had married Goldup sixteen years ago and in spite of the age gap (Jessie was twelve years older than her husband), they were happily married and went everywhere together. They had left Reading only a fortnight earlier to take up residence at Maidenhead.

Mr Long, noticing that Mrs Snow's husband's middle name was Jesse, and remembering that the note had blamed 'Jesse', asked her, 'Was your husband ever known as Jesse?' Mrs Snow replied that he was known as Charles, never as Jesse. Mr Long then asked, 'Was your sister known as Jesse?' to which Mrs Snow replied, 'Yes always.'

Mr Long then asked Mrs Snow, 'Did you and your husband lend the prisoner and his wife some money?' Mrs Snow replied that they had lent the Goldups some money and that they wanted it back; this situation, however, had not caused bad blood between them, they were still on the best of terms.

Cross-examined by Mr Clements for the defence Edith Snow stated that Goldup had lost £50 that he had invested in the bungalow. He had been, and was still, suffering from depression, she considered him mentally ill and said that he believed he had fumes and vapours around him and that they were choking him. In answer to another question from Mr Clements the witness stated that when she and Charles had visited the bungalow at White Waltham, Percy had taken her into the garden and described the choking vapours. He also told her the police were watching him and that everybody was against him. He also said that he would not be alive much longer. Neither the prosecution nor the defence having any more questions, Mrs Snow was allowed to take her seat.

Since the time of the offence, committed in April, Percy Goldup had remained in custody at Brixton prison. The next witness was Dr Watson, senior medical officer at that establishment. Dr Watson stated that in his opinion the prisoner was suffering from manic depression and insane melancholia. He had had long chats with Goldup and was sure that his

MAIDENHEAD BUNGALOW TRAGEDY.—The Heywood's Park bungalow, "Elms End," where a terrible discovery was made last week-end. Mrs. Jessie Goldup was found dead and her husband had extensive wounds in the throat. Their photographs are inset.
[Photo Greville, Maidenhead.]

Newspaper cutting on the Jessie Goldup tragedy

claim of amnesia since the event was genuine; when things became too unbearable the mind was inclined to blot them out totally. In answer to a question from Mr Long the doctor answered that in his long chats with the prisoner, Goldup had never mentioned any quarrel or jealousy between himself and his wife; as far as he (Watson) was concerned it was a harmonious marriage and Goldup was a devoted husband. Dr Watson stood down.

His place was taken by Mrs Maria Hipsey, a lady who kept a lodging house in Norfolk Road, Reading. Mrs Hipsey explained that Mr and Mrs Goldup had lodged with her between August 1928 and February 1929. She stated that Goldup had some strange ways that she found most uncanny. Things had steadily deteriorated until in late January her lodger started to accuse her of trying to chloroform him. At this point she had asked the couple to leave.

Mrs Hipsey's place was taken by Dr Michael F. Murphy of London

Street, Reading. Murphy informed the court that he was Goldup's local doctor and also that he had worked some years in a mental asylum. He thought that the prisoner was badly depressed and also mentally ill. In answer to a question from Mr Clements, Murphy informed the court that it was quite possible that in this condition Goldup could murder his wife and then remember nothing about it a short while afterwards.

At this point Mr Justice Shearman asked Dr Murphy to stand down. He then called learned counsel together and spoke to them briefly. Dismissing them he turned to the jury and directed them to bring a verdict of 'Guilty but insane'. This was quickly done and Justice Shearman then sentenced Percy Goldup to be detained during His Majesty's pleasure. The prisoner left the court weeping, a broken man who was destined to spend the remainder of his years in Broadmoor. A sad story indeed.

CHAPTER TWELVE

THE MURDER OF MRS GWEN WARREN BY ERNEST HUTCHINSON ON 11 OCTOBER 1932 AT MAIDENHEAD

Just three short years after the horrifying murder of Jessie Goldup in 1929, the good citizens of Maidenhead were once again thrust into the gratuitous headlines by a second murder. Once again in the Heywood's Park area, the scene of the blood-chilling crime was just a stone's throw from the bungalow of the ill-fated Goldups.

In 1932 Mrs Gwen Warren lived in Heywood's Park with her son Ronnie aged twelve and her daughter Constance who was just eighteen months. They shared a bungalow called Davyholme in Heywood Avenue on the Heywood's Park Estate.

Gwen Warren had experienced unsuccessful marriage with Thomas William Warren. They had separated some three years previously but had reunited shortly afterwards. The union, however, had not withstood the pressure and now Thomas Warren had returned to his native Burnham.

'Uncle Ernest' (Ernest Hutchinson), aged forty-two, was a native of the Midlands. He was 5 feet 7 inches tall, with ginger hair, and worked locally as a baker's roundsman. As is sometimes the way with lodgers, it was but a short step from the spare bedroom to that of the mistress of the house. However, Gwen Warren's favours were only to be bestowed upon the industrious, so when Ernest lost his job in August it would seem that he was relegated to his own bedroom. If you want the indulgence of a married man, bring home a married man's wage was the unspoken ultimatum.

With the loss of a job, and apparently little prospect of another, Ernest Hutchinson was opting for a short-term policy in answer to his problems; turning to the inevitable mainstay of the 1930s working class, he sought solace in the bottle.

On 10 September young Ronnie returned home from doing some errand to be told that arrangements had been made for him to stay with his aunt. Miss Fleet of Burnham. The lad was given his rail fare by 'Uncle Ernest' and quite happily set off for his aunt's abode in nearby Burnham.

On returning the following morning Ronnie was met by Hutchinson at the gate. He had little Constance in his arms and he placed her directly into her brother's care. 'Your mother's gone to Birmingham to see friends,' Hutchinson explained, 'You will have to take Connie to Burnham.' With this he turned, locking the boy outside the house, grabbed his coat and afterwards escorted Ronnie and his tiny sister part way to the station.

Miss Fleet was a little surprised to find the pair of waifs on her doorstep once again. This was unlike her sister Gwen, she and her children were usually inseparable, and when Ronnie explained his mother had gone to Birmingham Miss Fleet began to experience a sickly, nagging doubt that all was not well.

It would be difficult to ascertain whether Miss Fleet's worries were alleviated or aggravated by a postcard that arrived the next day (12 September); it was signed by Gwen and read 'Staying till Friday. Will write you so please keep Connie and Ronnie till then.'

The postcard seemed genuine, but it still left the younger sister with an uneasy feeling. She took Ronnie back to Heywood Avenue agreeing to keep Connie until Friday.

If Miss Fleet was uneasy she was not alone. It was a feeling shared by Mr Joseph Hutton, an ex-policeman who lived at number 8 next door to Davyholme in Heywood Avenue. Hutton had had several chats with Gwen Warren over the garden fence. She had seemed very nervous lately and had confided in him that she was scared stiff of Hutchinson and terrified to sleep at night. This somewhat alarmed Joseph Hutton but he thought that Gwen Warren was a little neurotic and in all probability exaggerating the danger she was in.

On 11 September, a Sunday, at 11 a.m., Hutton noticed Hutchinson in the garden. He enquired about Gwen, who was usually an early riser. 'She's still in bed,' replied Hutchinson. 'She's making a day of it.'

Monday 12 September found twelve-year-old Ronnie at home for the third time in as many days. He arrived at midday only to be told that he must once again return to his aunt's. Hutchinson explained that the boy could not possibly stay at home, as he himself was going to Birmingham to spend a few days with Ronnie's mother; they would both return on Friday. Hutchinson gave the boy a note to that effect and then once again escorted him to the railway station.

The note Miss Fleet received ran as follows: 'Dear Miss Fleet, Just a few lines to you saying I am going to Birmingham to Gwen for a few days so no use writing to her until Friday. Keep Ronnie and Connie till then.'

On the same day, 12 September, a Maidenhead second-hand dealer from Bridge Street paid Hutchinson £3 16s for a piano, a sofa and a kitchen table, all of which were delivered by hand-cart.

Meanwhile at Burnham Miss Fleet was becoming more and more alarmed. The note she received from the ever-returning Ronnie was the final straw. Miss Rachel Fleet gathered up Connie and she and Ronnie once again headed for Heywood's Park.

On arrival they found the house closed, the doors locked and bolted. Miss Fleet swiftly called on the nextdoor neighbour Joseph Hutton. Appreciating and sharing the woman's anxiety, Hutton helped Ronnie through the larder window. The boy thereupon opened the back door allowing Miss Fleet and Hutton entry.

It was Hutton who found Gwen Warren's body under a mattress in the front bedroom. Miss Fleet went to pieces; the sisters had been very close. She was deeply indebted to the experience of Joseph Hutton that enabled him to take full control of the situation. The police from Maidenhead were contacted and through them the police doctor, Dr Wilson, who stated that the body was fully clothed and that there were no signs of violence.

The next day, 13 September, a post-mortem was held at Maidenhead under the jurisdiction of the local coroner Mr Sutchberry. Dr Wilson estimated that death had occurred some four days previously but said that he could not reveal the cause of Mrs Warren's demise until the vital organs had been returned from analysis.

By this time the newspapers had got hold of the facts and there was a hue and cry for Ernest Hutchinson. His description was circulated to many police forces and, as in all such cases, there were many false sightings. One well-publicized mis-sighting was at Pangbourne, where a local police inspector commandeered an irate motorist's vehicle and gave chase to an unidentified ginger-headed man along the river bank.

More sightings were reported in Birmingham, a city where the local police did have some expectancy of Hutchinson surfacing. However, none of the follow-ups came to fruition.

When Ernest Hutchinson was finally apprehended at Southend on 16 September, the arrest came through a tip-off from Scotland Yard to Essex police. The Essex constabulary surrounded a cheap boarding house where a couple were identified as Hutchinson and a lady of dubious repute, one Doris Dew of Kennington, London.

There was no struggle as Ernest Hutchinson was taken to Southend police station by Detective Inspector Harris. Hutchinson's only words to the local officer were 'I knew she was there but I didn't do it'. Hutchinson was informed of his rights and also told that he would be transferred to Maidenhead where an Inspector Barrett wished to interview him with reference to the death of Mrs Gwen Warren.

Hutchinson turned to Detective Inspector Harris with what seemed to be surprise, 'I know the woman and used to live with her, but surely the police don't expect I did it.' Later at Maidenhead, Hutchinson gave a full statement to Inspector Barrett, the gist of which was as follows.

Ernest Hutchinson admitted he had argued with Gwen Warren on the Saturday, the argument being about his being out of work and also his incessant smoking. By bedtime they had made up their differences and Hutchinson had been in bed for some minutes when Gwen came in and took off her nightdress. She then left the room; Hutchinson supposed this was to tease him. Gwen then told him that she had no intention of sleeping with him. Hutchinson had told her to please herself and later gone into a light sleep. At midnight he woke to hear her footsteps going downstairs (he was later to add that he thought Gwen had at least one other boyfriend as he had found a stranger's hat downstairs). On the Sunday morning he made a cup of tea and took it into Ronnie's room but the boy was not there. He then went into the front bedroom and saw Gwen's stockinged feet protruding from under several mattresses. Hutchinson then pulled up the mattresses and saw that his beloved Gwen was dead. He could tell that someone had been in the house and he surmised that it had been either Gwen's unknown lover or her ex-husband Tommy Warren who had been threatening to do her an injury for some time.

Hutchinson then stated that he had panicked and instead of reporting her death to the police he had spun a yarn to the neighbours with the hope of covering things up. He understood that he had behaved like an idiot, but he was a fool and not a murderer.

On Tuesday 4 October, Ernest Hutchinson appeared at Maidenhead police court charged with the murder of Gwendoline Anne Warren. For the prosecution was Mr G.R. Paling and the defence was in the hands of Mr Woodward from High Wycombe. The trial had attracted a crowd, many of whom were there to see Sir Bernard Spilsbury, the world-famous pathologist.

The trial was relatively brief but it included some pretty damning evidence from Dr Wilson who stated that Gwen Warren had been struck on the head with a hammer but that this had not killed her; she had met her demise through asphyxiation caused by the pile of mattresses forced on top of her.

Sir Bernard Spilsbury concurred fully with Dr Wilson's conclusions; he also stated that the victim's fingernails were vivid which was a common sign of asphyxiation. His autopsy had discovered bruises on the head which were probably received a few minutes before death. Shortly afterwards Hutchinson was formally charged and committed to Reading Assizes on 14 October.

The trial at Reading was before Mr Justice McKinnon. For the prosecution was Mr Earingey KC. Hutchinson's defence was handled by Mr St John-Micklethwaite KC who was ably assisted by Mr Cockburn.

The prosecution's first witness was the victim's husband Thomas Warren. He informed the court that he had no longer any interest in his wife's goings-on and certainly no longer bore her any malice. Warren stated that he had lived with Gwen at 4 Court View, Maidenhead, until 10 June that year. At that time she had taken the children and left him. In answer to a question from the prosecution Warren replied that the accused had come to him as a lodger in July 1930. Warren was also sure that Connie was the accused's daughter and not his. Thomas Warren had a foolproof alibi for the night of the murder and had at no time deliberately approached his wife. He said that he considered himself well rid of her.

With this the prosecution's next witness was called, the second-hand dealer from Bridge Street. He witnessed that Hutchinson had sold him the items from the Warren household on 12 September. Ex-policeman and neighbour Joseph Hutton witnessed how Gwen Warren had told him that with Hutchinson in the house she was too worried to sleep. He also described how he entered the house with Miss Fleet and Ronnie. Hutton followed this with some disastrous evidence as far as Hutchinson was concerned. He told of his conversation with the accused in the back garden on Sunday 11 Semptember. Hutton had asked how Mrs Warren was and Hutchinson had insisted she was still in bed.

Miss Doris Dew, the lady of dubious vocation, was next to take the stand. She announced that she had been introduced to Hutchinson in London and had travelled with him to a Southend lodging house where they had stayed as man and wife. Hutchinson had given her a jumper and two necklaces; these items had since been identified as belonging to Gwen Warren. Miss Dew had been shocked when the accused had been arrested the following morning.

Miss Dew did not give the appearance of a lady who would be easily shocked, but finding her room surrounded by police early in the morning must have been a little disconcerting.

After Doris Dew stood down, Hutchinson took the stand in a hushed court-room. Hutchinson's long oratory was very much an elaboration of his written statement to the police; there was, however, a somewhat altered ending. He was sure that Gwen had not slept with him that night because she was meeting someone else in the other bedroom. Whomever this rendezvous was with, it was certainly a man. Hutchinson said that it was this man who had killed her as he slept in the master bedroom. He had discovered the body in the morning and had been so distressed that he had reacted as in a trance. He remembered the front door latch was down so somebody could easily have come and gone.

Justice McKinnon then asked Hutchinson if he was really suggesting that somebody came in that night and killed her, to which Hutchinson agreed. His lordship then asked the accused why he had not contacted the police. 'I was too upset,' came his reply. McKinnon then remonstrated with the accused, suggesting that Hutchinson was not too upset to sell Mrs Warren's possessions and pick up a prostitute. Mr Earingey pursued this line of questioning for a brief period and then concluded the case for the prosecution. The trial was adjourned until the following Saturday morning.

DECLARATION OF SHERIFF

AND OTHERS

(31 Vict. Cap. 24)

We, the undersigned, hereby declare that Judgement of Death was this Day executed on ERNEST HUTCHINSON in His Majesty's Prison of OXFORD in our presence.

Dated this 23rd day of NOVEMBER 1932.

G H Palmer Sheriff of BERKSHIRE

_____ Justice of the Peace

_____ for_____

E C W Richards Governor of the said Prison.

D K Slater-Hunt Chaplain of the said Prison.

Sheriff's declaration of the execution of Ernest Hutchinson

On Saturday 15 October Justice McKinnon began his summing-up. He pointed out that there was one fact that was undeniable. That some time between the night of 10 September and the morning of 11 September at the house in Heywood Avenue, the woman met her death. The prosecution ask you to say it was murder.

His lordship went on to point out that on the day when Hutchinson had known of Mrs Warren's death he had embarked upon a course of lies to everybody about it. He had told her closest relatives and neighbours that she had gone to Birmingham, he had sold her furniture, and appropriated the money. Taking his proceeds he had journeyed to London and obtained the services of a prostitute, giving her the dead woman's trinkets. The pair had travelled to Southend where Hutchinson was finally arrested by the police.

The judge also reminded the jury of Hutchinson's opening statement when first detained which was 'As they were bound to get me sooner or later, I decided to have as good a time as possible'. Mentioning

E READING STANDARD. SATURDAY

MURDER TRIAL IN READING

Sentence of Death Passed on Maidenhead Baker.

HOW ACCUSED RECEIVED THE VERDICT.

As he entered the dock at the Berkshire Assizes on Friday arraigned for the murder of Gwendoline Annie Warren, 36, a married woman, of Heywood Avenue, White Waltham, Maidenhead, who had been living apart from her husband, Ernest Hutchinson, 42, a baker, looked round the court and smiled. Throughout the trial his attitude was one of apparent unconcern, and during the hearing of the evidence he frequently smiled. He was quite unmoved when the grim and sordid details of the discovery of the unhappy woman's body hidden in a bedroom was related. On Saturday afternoon Hutchinson smiled when the jury returned the verdict of guilty, and he laughed softly as Mr. Justice MacKinnon passed sentence of death. The Judge's voice shook with emotion, but Hutchinson, as he heard his doom pronounced, smiled broadly, and was still smiling as he left the dock.

The trial aroused a good deal of interest, and large crowds have assembled each day outside the Assize Courts. Many who were unable to obtain admission waited outside to hear the result of the trial and to watch the departure of the Judge. Inside the crowded Court was a fair sprinkling of women.

THE FINAL SCENES.

Mr. W. G. Earengey, K.C., and Mr. Ralph Thomas appeared for the Crown, while prisoner, who pleaded not guilty, was represented by Mr. St. J. Gore Micklethwait, K.C. the Recorder for Reading, and Mr. A. W. Cockburn (instructed by Mr. E. Woodward, of High Wycombe).

Opening the case for the Crown, Mr. Earengey said that the murdered woman was the wife of William Thomas Warren, of Burnham, Bucks. In July, 1920, Hutchinson went to the Warren's house as a lodger. On June 10th of this year Mrs. Warren parted from her husband and went to Heywood Avenue with her two children, Ronald, aged 12, and a 16-months old baby girl, Constance, to live with Hutchinson. Mrs. Warren was apparently last seen alive on the evening of Saturday, September 11th. Ronald was not there as he had gone to visit his aunt, Miss Fleet, a schoolmistress at Burnham. When the boy arrived home on the Sunday Hutchinson told him that his mother had gone away. The boy slept with Hutchinson that night and the next day he was sent with his baby sister to Miss

This concluded the hearing of the evidence on Friday, and the Court adjourned until the following morning. The jury of nine men and three women, under the care of a police officer, and a woman bailiff, stayed the night at the Ship Hotel. They spent the evening playing cards." On Saturday morning they went to a looked room in another part of the Court and inspected the bedstead on which Mrs. Warren's body was found.

The atmosphere in the Court was tense when the closing stages of the trial began.

AN UNSUPPORTED THEORY.

Making his final speech for the Crown, Mr. Earengey submitted that there was no possibility of manslaughter. Prisoner's own story was inconsistent with the theory of manslaughter, for he said he knew nothing of the happenings on that fateful night. Even if the woman had fallen on to the bed unconscious the jury would have to to consider who piled more than a hundredweight of clothing and other articles on top of her—a mass of material which probably caused her death from suffocation.

Newspaper cutting of the Ernest Hutchinson trial

Hutchinson's evidence that someone else had done the deed, with a strong inference that the man suggested was Warren, Justice McKinnon treated this with scorn. He pointed out that it was quite obvious that Thomas Warren had ceased to care tuppence about his wife's activities.

Mr Justice McKinnon's summing-up ended at 1.45; the jury were out for an hour and ten minutes before they returned with a verdict of guilty. Hutchinson watched unflinchingly as the judge placed the black cap on his head. As the death sentence was passed the prisoner broke into a joyless laugh which the court would hear continued as he was lead away to the cells.

There was an appeal two weeks later at the Court of Criminal Appeal in London, at which Hutchinson was represented by Mr Cockburn. The appeal was held on the grounds that Justice McKinnon had misdirected the jury and also that certain questions contravened the 1898 Criminal Evidence Act, but their lordships, led by Lord Chief Justice Heward, were having none of it. The appeal was dismissed.

Hutchinson was returned to Oxford to spend the remainder of his days in a condemned cell. The good people of Maidenhead did not deem it appropriate to raise a petition so Ernest Hutchinson was hanged at 8 a.m. on Wednesday 23 November 1932. The hangman was Alfred Allen of Wolverhampton who was officiating for the first time. The execution would seem to have gone successfully and the notice was pinned on the prison gates at 8.15, following which the small crowd moved slowly away.

CHAPTER THIRTEEN

THE MURDER OF FREDERICK JAMES PAUL AT WINKFIELD, FEBRUARY 1939

Frederick James Paul was a local character, and at eighty-five he was still fit and hearty. Originally a native of Weymouth, he had moved into the village of Winkfield many years before. Fred was a market gardener in a very small way. He lived in the village; his bungalow, now reduced to one room (the roof of the other having collapsed), was adjacent to the small nursery from which Fred gleaned his living. The old gardener was quite content with his lot, one room was sufficient for his scant belongings. He was out most of the day either tending his frugal crops or selling them in Windsor and Maidenhead. He slept in the one armchair and while he enjoyed company he preferred a semi-isolated existence. His spartan needs were easily affordable from the one-man business.

Windsor Bridge, where 85-year-old Fred Paul sold the meagre produce of his Winkfield nursery

The Tally Ho, now a private house; farm labourer William Coombs heard several shots coming from the direction of the Tally Ho on Thursday 9 February. (Photograph by P. Bourne)

It was a combination of the last two factors that, in all probability, cost the old man his life. It was rumoured that he had a substantial cache hidden away, saved from years of frugal living. It was also known that he lived in virtual isolation.

On Wednesday 8 February at 7 a.m. postman Frederick Godfrey delivered a letter to the nursery and spent several minutes chewing the fat with the old man. He found old Fred jocular and friendly as always. On Thursday 9 February Godfrey made another delivery to Fred's abode but could not get an answer. This was not unusual, the old man was often out and about very early.

That night, between 11 and 11.30 p.m., farm labourer William Coombs of Crouch Lane, Winkfield, heard gunshots from the direction of the Tally Ho public house, which was situated very near to Mr Paul's nursery. This again was not unusual, in a country district inundated with large estates where half the population were either poacher or gamekeeper.

On Friday 10 February postman Godfrey had no deliveries for the nursery. The local newspaper boy had, however, but noticed nothing amiss as he pushed Fred's paper through the letterbox at 7.30 a.m.

There was something amiss, though, when Mr Albert Gray, a butcher's roundsman, delivered some meat at 11 a.m. The door was always ajar so Gray pushed it a little further so that he could deposit his order inside. The room was in extreme disarray. Drawers had been pulled out and their contents littered the floor. On the wall in the corner were traces of spattered blood, and there was also a damp pool of blood on the threadbare carpet. Unbelievably, the butcher's roundsman placed his order on the table then closed the door and left without further inspection or notifying the authorities.

At 12.15 Reg Stone, a delivering coalman, did make a further inspection after noticing lamps alight at that time of day. He inspected the disarray of the room and the blood. He then made full speed to Winkfield police station.

PC Coombs arrived at The Nursery, Tally Ho Lane, Winkfield at 1 p.m. He made his way through the debris of Fred Paul's one-roomed dwelling. It was obvious to his experienced eye that the room had been ransacked in the execution of a frenzied search rather than suffering vandalism. Coombs's fear of foul play was endorsed by the discovery of the bloody stains and a pair of broken spectacles in the corner of the room. The young constable tracked the bloodstains and scuffed grass from the back of the dwelling to a small pool, a distance of some 80 yards. There he encountered a sight that would have intimidated the stoutest of hearts. The body of Fred Paul lay partly submerged in the shallow pool. Only the head and shoulders were discernible from the murky surface. The skull and part of the neck had been blasted away leaving vast gaps in the countenance.

Coombs sent for assistance which arrived within the hour in the form of Superintendent Braby of Wokingham, accompanied by several constables. The body was removed to the dwelling. It was found to be fully clothed except for a jacket. The hip pocket of the trousers had been pulled out (it was later to emerge that Fred Paul was known to carry a fair amount of cash in his hip pocket from which he paid all his bills). The other pockets, when searched by PC Edgar Clark, were found to contain 4s 8d in change.

One of Superintendent Braby's first actions was to have the shallow pool pumped dry. This revealed Paul's jacket which was turned inside out and gave the impression of having been searched. Unfortunately for Braby his expectations were dashed when the draining revealed no weapon. However, beside the pool was a damp patch of blood which was probably where the murderer rested the body before heaving it into the water. Also two cartridge wads were discovered close by.

At midday on Saturday 11 February the body was examined by Dr James Vernon of Ascot. The doctor stated that Mr Paul had been shot twice, once in the temple and once in the neck. Either shot had been sufficient to kill him.

Superintendent Braby was trying to drag the different components of the case together. He already had a suspect, a man who had worked for Fred Paul on a temporary basis many times. A man who had charged the old man for using his ferrets to rid the nursery of rats, a man who had many small financial dealings with Fred Paul, albeit a couple of years ago. This same man must have been paid out of the hip pocket on numerous occasions. Braby also knew that the suspect made his own shot and used ICI cartridges and bullets similar to those that had been found on the body. This same man had been witnessed in the vicinity that fatal day and he had also been heard to tell of Fred Paul's 'long sock' at the local taverns.

Braby stayed his hand, however. A coroner's inquest opened at Ascot police station on Tuesday 14 February before Mr R.S. Payne of Reading. Evidence produced endorsed the theory that this was definitely murder and not suicide. Medical evidence finally proved suicide to be impossible.

The body was identified by Mr Walter Paul, the victim's son. Paul also informed the inquiry that his father possessed no firearms. Further evidence was given by the various callers at Fred Paul's address from Wednesday 8 February until the discovery of the body on Friday 10 February.

Dr Vernon gave an exact report on the cause of death. The time of death was placed at between 10 and 12 p.m. on Thursday 9 February, this being arrived at by the temperature and state of the body. This was, however, an inexact science so this point was left open to question. It was obvious that the murder had been at night because of the lamps still being alight; William Coombs's evidence of hearing shots from that direction at between 11 and 11.30 p.m. pinpointed the time of death neatly as far as the police were concerned.

Superintendent Braby informed the court that enquiries were going well and that he hoped for a preliminary hearing soon. Mr Payne adjourned the proceedings until 9 March. He also directed that the body should be taken to the Royal Berkshire Hospital.

In the evening of Thursday 14 February Braby, accompanied by PC Coombs, arrested George Henry Willis at his home, 5 Braywick Cottages, Ascot. In reply to the charge of the murder of Frederick Paul, Willis replied, 'I am not guilty, my conscience is clear.' He was then removed to Ascot police station. Also removed by the police were a number of items including rubber gloves, a 4.10 shotgun, a quantity of shot, powder, wadding and cartridge cases. They also took away a pair of tweezers.

On Wednesday 15 February Willis appeared at Ascot police station before Mr A.P. Shaw. He once again pleaded not guilty and was remanded until the preliminary hearing.

The preliminary hearing opened on 10 March at Windsor Guildhall, an unlikely venue with few facilities. There was no dock and so Willis spent the entire proceedings sitting on an open bench alongside various people involved in the case. Mr A.P. Shaw again presided; the prosecution was represented by Mr G.R. Paling, the defence by Mr E.R. Guest.

Once again, much detail involving the finding of the body was related, but there was also a lengthy description by Superintendent Braby of the arrest, the circumstances, and the items that had been removed from the Willis residence. Braby described how at the scene of the arrest, his officers had found powder, wadding and shot very similar to those found at the scene of the crime. It was obvious that Willis made his own ammunition from components manufactured by ICI, which were the same as those found at the Winkfield Nursery. Braby also stated that when questioned on this point Willis had said that he had purchased the ammunition from a man named Ayres at Easthampstead. When questioned, Ayres had denied this.

When asked whether he had been near Winkfield, Willis had replied that he had not been there for over a year. The same Mr Ayres, however, had informed the police that Willis and he regularly cut through Winkfield on their way to Bracknell.

Superintendent Braby continued, informing the hearing of how Willis had done odd jobs for Fred Paul. He obviously knew the layout of the

The preliminary hearing into the death of Frederick Paul was heard at the unsuitable venue of Windsor Guildhall. The facilities were few, there was no dock and the accused had to sit on a bench alongside others involved in the case.
(Photograph by P. Bourne)

nursery, and he must often have been paid from Paul's hip pocket. Braby went on to state that witnesses had heard Willis mention in pubs that Fred Paul had a 'long stocking', this being the local jargon meaning a lot of money hidden away.

The superintendent then went on to mention other aspects of the case. A butler and a boot boy from Foliejon Park had seen Willis near the nursery on 9 February. Later Mr Paling produced the butler and asked him to point

A butler and a boot boy from Foliejon Park deposed that they had seen Willis near Paul's nursery on 9 February 1939. (Photograph by P. Bourne)

out the man he had seen but the defence objected to this, and the objection was sustained. The superintendent informed the inquiry that Willis had no alibi for 9 February other than that he had been at home in bed.

Finally Mr Braby came to the tweezers which had been found among a lot of clock parts at 5 Braywick Cottages; they had belonged to Mr Fred Paul and he would prove that they had been in his possession shortly before his murder. They were unusual because one blade had been broken, filed and then flattened. With this the superintendent stood down. His evidence was followed by that of Mr Walter Paul who deposed that he recognized the tweezers as his father's and also that he had heard Willis state in several pubs that his father had a 'long stocking'.

The easiest and least complicated way of dealing with George Henry Willis's defence evidence is to do a precis of the more salient points. In answer to Superintendent Braby's accusations proffered by Mr Paling, George Willis had stated that he had known Fred Paul for a number of years and had often worked for him, ratting and cutting pea-sticks and the

The White Hart at Winkfield, thought to be one of the establishments in which Willis boasted of Fred Paul's 'long stocking'. (Photograph by P. Bourne)

like, but he had not worked for Fred or been near the nursery for over two years. He would admit, however, that he and Ayres had sometimes walked through Winkfield en route to Bracknell.

Willis also stated that he did not make his own ammunition; if he had not purchased it from Ayres then he had purchased it from one of many other suppliers in the neighbourhood. ICI components were not uncommon. In answer to questions about his belief in Fred Paul's 'long stocking', Willis swore that that was an expression that he never used and he certainly had not mentioned it in a pub, especially in front of Mr Walter Paul.

Willis claimed that the two men who said they had seen him in the vicinity of Tally Ho Lane at 5 p.m. on 9 February were grossly mistaken. Also that the tweezers had been in his possession since 1932, and had been given to him with a load of old clock parts by old Mrs Norton of Binfield.

Willis stated that his reason for not having an alibi was because he was innocent and didn't think he needed one. On the evening of 8 February a Miss Rapley had come to see him from Fifield. They had talked for a while

The Stag and Hounds, Braywick, where George Willis was drinking on 9 February 1939. (Photograph by P. Bourne)

and at about 8.30 p.m. she had caught the bus home. Willis cycled after it and they had chatted again near her home. He had then cycled home about 10.30 and had gone to bed. On 9 February Willis had spent the day gardening, finishing at 5 p.m. He had walked to The Stag and Hounds at Braywick; returning home at 8.30 he had gone straight to bed.

George Willis concluded his evidence in the mid-afternoon. The inquiry decided that there was a case to answer and remanded Willis to Reading Assizes.

The trial of George Willis was held on 14 May 1939 at Reading Assizes and lasted two days. It was enacted before the High Sheriff of Berkshire, Mr L.A. Wroughton. Mr Justice Charles presided. For the prosecution were Mr W.H. Cartwright-Sharp KC and Mr H.H. Madocks. Representing the accused were Mr A.J. Long KC and Mr E.R. Guest.

Much of the evidence had already been thoroughly aired on three previous occasions, but at an assizes there is an added atmosphere of intensity coupled with austerity. There were, however, several new pieces of evidence, two favouring the prosecution and two favouring the defence.

Mr Arthur Dunsford, butler at Foliejon Park, stated that at 5 p.m. on 9 February the telephone had been found to be out of order so his mistress had instructed him to bicycle down to South Lodge. On his journey he got off his bicycle to cross a cattle grid when he noticed a man with a ferocious and haggard expression standing there. He had bid the man good day but had received no reply. He now recognized the man as the prisoner. The boot boy who had followed the butler with a further message also witnessed and recognized the prisoner.

'Are you absolutely sure this is the same man?' demanded Mr Long. 'Yes, sir,' replied Dunsford. 'At twilight time, on a drizzly night, with only a fleeting glimpse as you passed by. Can you be certain this is the man?' asked Long. 'Yes, sir,' came the not so confident reply.

Dr G. Roche-Lynch, a ballistics expert, took the stand. He stated that the bullets that had been taken from the body were composed of a particularly soft lead identical to the lead found in 5 Braywick Cottages. 'Was not this lead of a common type found all over the country?' enquired Mr Long. 'No, it is unusual,' came the reply. 'Very unusual or a little unusual?' queried Long. 'It is not the usual type of lead,' the doctor answered.

Dr Roche-Lynch had also inspected the tweezers. He said they were also unusual. He had tried many public shops but had been unable to purchase a pair that resembled them. 'They are unusual because they have a broken and splayed blade,' suggested Mr Long. 'They are of an unusual design, notwithstanding that,' answered Dr Roche-Lynch. 'But commodities that are unusual today may have been quite commonplace some twenty years ago,' suggested Mr Long.

Later Mr John Norton of Binfield was to identify the tweezers as some his mother had given to Willis in 1932 with some watch and clock innards. He stated that they had been in his mother's possession many years prior to that. The tweezers were rapidly becoming the focal point of the whole trial.

Mr Cartwright-Sharp vehemently attacked Willis on the stand. 'How long have these tweezers been in your possession?' he asked. 'Since 1932,' came the reply. 'How do you explain that they match a pair that poor Fred Paul possessed shortly before his death?' Willis replied that he couldn't explain this and when asked how the blade became broken said, 'It was broken when I was given them.' 'How did it become beaten and flattened?'

'I did it myself, I used them as a screwdriver for watch repairs.' When asked why he had done this Willis said that he did not have a small enough screwdriver so he made one. Cartwright-Sharp asked Willis to demonstrate how he used them.

It was one of the most strained and dramatic periods of any trial in the history of English justice. The court stood hushed to a man as the clerk placed an open-backed watch before the prisoner. Refusing the assistance of an eyeglass Willis deftly took the tweezers in his right hand, then skilfully and efficiently extracted three tiny screws from the back of the watch. The deathly hush continued, the silence broken only by three tiny ringing noises as the prisoner deposited the screws one by one on the dock. Willis's hands had not shaken, his expression not changed during the performance; then he solemnly handed the implement back to the clerk.

Mr Cartwright-Sharp's speech made a lot of reference to coincidence. Did the jury not find it a coincidence that the cartridges were the same, the lead was the same and the wadding the same? Also he thought it had been proved that the tweezers were the same. Why had Willis lied about purchasing the ammunition from Ayres? Why had he no alibi? Could the jury accept that so many unfortunate coincidences had been experienced by one man?

To Mr Long's idea the prosecution had established nothing at all. Bodies immersed in water gave very varied indications as to the time of death. William Coombs's gunshots could easily have been fired by poachers; the court was not even sure which evening Mr Paul had died. He admitted that Mr Paul had been beaten before he died and was probably lying on the ground when shot. Mr Long believed he had probably been shot with a revolver of the same bore as that used by Willis; it was fairly commonplace.

The evidence of the firearm and of the ammunition was contradictory. First they were both very popular and common, but a man would have to be an absolute idiot not to dispose of them after the event.

The eye-witnesses were very suspect. It was nearly dark, rain was falling and they received the most fleeting of glimpses. Even so they could only place the person they had seen somewhere near Tally Ho Lane on one of the days in question. There must have been hundreds of people in the vicinity.

The tweezers had been in Willis's possession for some time, that was proved by his dexterity with them. Notwithstanding the fact that the tweezers were Willis's, could the jury really believe that in the middle of the most heinous of crimes, the perpetrator would stop to pick up a twopenny-halfpenny pair of broken tweezers and then leave them about his abode to incriminate himself. Mr Long thought not.

Summing up, Mr Justice Charles described the case as the most brutal he had come across in eleven years on the bench. He had obviously been impressed by Willis's example with the tweezers in court. Looking straight at the jury he questioned, could a man commit such an abhorrent crime and then in a crowded court-room, while on trial for his life, use the implements once owned by the deceased without showing any emotion.

Mr Justice Charles continued, 'The chain of evidence, like any other chain, is as strong as its weakest link. It is no good having strong links interposed with weak links. The jury must ask itself if there are any weak links in this case.'

After a quarter of an hour the jury decided there were too many weak links and George Henry Willis walked away a free man.

CHAPTER FOURTEEN

THE MURDER OF MRS EDITH PRICKET AT TILEHURST, 1939

At the same Berkshire Assizes where Willis had displayed his dispassionate calm and a coolness that ultimately brought about his release, another case of murder was examined.

It was unique for the good folk of Berkshire to have two men charged with the ultimate crime at the one assizes. The second trial, a crime that modern police might call a domestic, lacked the passion and flare of the first. It did, however, give the public a second chance to experience Mr A.J. Long KC at his eloquent and unrivalled best.

To say that some of the neighbours of the Prickets in Rodway Road were a little disenchanted with them would be an understatement. The rows between Sydney Pricket and his wife were regular, loud and volatile. The couple lived at number 44; their closest neighbour, therefore the one most affected by these affrays, was Mrs Rebecca Izzard at number 42. Mrs Izzard had heard Edith Pricket being threatened by her husband on many occasions since Christmas, 1938. The rows had grown in intensity through the new year, in fact 14, 15 and 16 January had been one continuous quarrel, rising and falling in intensity, brief respites occurring only when one or other combatant was out of the house.

Mrs Izzard knew that 39-year-old Sydney was insanely jealous and lived with the paranoid fixation that his wife was about to leave him. Last Armistice Day Edith Pricket had taken some flowers to place on her father's grave, she had been less than an hour overdue in returning and Sydney Pricket had visited Mrs Izzard three times. Each time he had been more stressed and each time he had asked her if she thought his wife had left him.

On the other side of the road, at number 65, Mrs Brenda Dunn was also having a tough time from Sydney Pricket. Apart from suffering from the noise of the rows, as several others in the vicinity did, Pricket had also decided that Brenda was his wife's confidante. This was partially true for Edith had often intimated to her friend that she was scared that Sydney was going insane.

Both Mrs Izzard and Mrs Dunn heard terrible, but not unusual, screams coming from number 44 on 16 January. They had also witnessed Sydney fleeing the house about 10.30 a.m.

PC Selwood received a call at Eldon borough police station at 10.45 a.m. on 16 January 1939. The call came from a local police box and was from a man who was obviously in a very distressed condition. 'Go to 44 Rodway Road,' the shaky voice instructed. PC Selwood tried to ascertain the caller's name and address. Ignoring the officer's requests the voice continued, 'Send an officer to 44 Rodway Road. I've lost my head.'

PC Selwood asked what the caller meant by this and the reply came: 'Go to my address and find out.' In spite of Selwood's procrastinations, attempting to detain the caller, the phone was replaced.

The young constable communicated through another police box to PC Trotman of the CID. Trotman proceeded to police box 12 where the original phone call had come from. On arrival Trotman discovered a man leaning against the railings near the box. He looked white and ill and he was shaking uncontrollably. Trotman sat the man down in the police box and tried to calm him while he took notes.

The constable discovered, with some difficulty, that the man's name was Sydney Pricket. In a stammering and faltering exposition Pricket informed Trotman: 'I have done in my wife. We've quarrelled for eight years and I couldn't stand it any more. I couldn't swallow it so I done her in.'

PC Trotman used the police box to call for assistance; he was shortly joined by Detective Inspector F.A. Knight and Detective Sergeant Lawrence. Turning to the inspector in a much calmer manner, Pricket enquired: 'May I see my solicitor Mr Berry? I know I shall be hung.'

Detective Inspector Knight travelled to 44 Rodway Road, Tilehurst. The door was unlocked so he entered the premises to find the body of Edith Pricket in the bedroom. She was lying on the bed; there were pressure marks around her throat. A blood spit about the size of half-a-crown was staining the pillow and there were further traces of blood on a man's crumpled pyjama jacket. There would seem to have been no evidence of a struggle.

Sending a message to Dr Murphy, the Reading police surgeon, Knight waited for his arrival before returning to the borough police station. There he charged Sydney Herbert Pricket with the wilful murder of his wife Edith Alice Pricket.

The coroner's inquest the following day was a brief affair. PC Timms of Reading police had the unenviable task of identifying the body. Edith Pricket had previously been Edith Timms, the constable's sister. Timms stated that Edith had been married to Pricket for some seven years.

Dr Michael Francis Murphy deposed that he had carried out a post-mortem examination with Dr Eric Gardner of Weybridge mortuary present. The doctors had agreed that death had been caused by asphyxia, brought about by homicidal manual strength. Any charges against Pricket were held over to the preliminary hearing.

The preliminary hearing was heard at Reading on 24 January 1939. The bench consisted of no fewer than six local JPs. Alderman Miss E.M. Sutton chaired, assisted by Lady Franklin-Silky, Mrs Cusden, H.T. Morely Esq., Noel Sutton Esq., and F. Adlam Esq. Mr E.G. Robey appeared for the prosecution, the defence was handled by Mr E.R. Guest.

The stately town of Reading was shocked by the news of the Pricket murder.
(Photograph by courtesy of Berkshire County Library)

Much evidence was heard from the prosecution about the rows at Rodway Road. Sworn testaments were read out by various neighbours, also by police officers who had been called on several occasions to the house. The police evidence, presented by Superintendent Osborne, was somewhat extensive.

Mr Guest was uneasy over whether Sydney Pricket should take the stand, but he decided to let him do so. Pricket would say nothing but that he had found a letter in his wife's pocket addressed to another man. Mr Guest informed the court that his client was mentally ill and asked for an adjournment to the assizes in four months' time. He hoped by then to have accrued considerably more data concerning Pricket's sanity. The adjournment was granted.

Guest also requested that his client should not be remanded in prison as it was obvious that he was psychiatrically ill. After some consultation with the clerk of the court Alderman Miss Sutton remanded the prisoner to Brixton where a psychiatric unit was in existence.

On 16 May at Reading Assizes the case was opened before Mr Justice Charles. For the prosecution was Mr John Foster KC, for the defence (fresh from their impressive vindication of George Willis) were Mr E.R. Guest and Mr A.J. Long KC. Sydney Pricket entered a plea of guilty but insane. Neither the facts of the crime nor the identity of the perpetrator were in dispute. As to the interpretation of whether Sydney Pricket had been insane at the time of these actions, there certainly was an abyss of conjecture.

The prosecution introduced Mr H.A. Grierson, an eminent psychiatrist, the head of the Brixton unit. Grierson stated that Pricket had been under his care since 25 January. His experience of the prisoner's behaviour was that he was rational and a loner who kept himself to himself although he often spoke of his unhappy marriage.

Mr Long in cross-examination asked Dr Grierson if he thought Sydney Pricket to be sane in the accepted sense of the word. Dr Grierson replied in the affirmative. Mr Long then asked if the information that Pricket had a first cousin in Broadmoor, that he had attempted to take his own life and that he was obsessed with childish literature would influence the good doctor's opinion.

Mr Long suggested to the psychiatrist that Pricket did not know what he was doing at the time of the murder. 'He did know what he was doing, I

Broadmoor Asylum, the ultimate destination of Sydney Herbert Pricket

have no doubt. He had told me so,' replied Grierson. 'He might have known what he had done afterwards, but that doesn't mean to say he knew what he was doing at the time,' said Long, to which Grierson replied, 'No one can know what a man was thinking at the time of a crime, but there is certainly no evidence to suggest that Pricket did not know what he was doing at the time.'

Mr Long, convinced that he might lose a battle of words with a specialized expert, decided to go for overkill by subjecting the court to a barrage of witnesses. Edith Maud Lavingdon née Pricket, informed the court that her husband, Sydney Pricket's cousin, was in Broadmoor for attempted suicide in 1919. Dr Arthur Bennett deposed that in 1926 he had been called to see Sydney Pricket who had cut his own throat. He made out an order for him to attend the Basingstoke psychiatric unit. Dr Digby Sanderland of Westminster testified that between 24 July and 2 August 1929 Pricket signed himself into a London psychiatric hospital on a voluntary basis.

Cyril Ernest House, relieving officer of Reading Corporation, stated that on 1 July 1938 he had found Pricket weeping. Pricket had said he wanted his wife. House had Pricket removed to Battle Hospital mental ward. Mr Eric Berry, a solicitor who had known Pricket for a number of years, informed the court that he considered him of too low intelligence to simulate insanity successfully.

Sydney Pricket made a very brief appearance. When asked by Mr Foster why he had killed his wife he replied that Edith was trying to irritate him so that she could divorce him under the new Matrimonial Act. Pricket was then asked to stand down.

After a brief summing-up by Mr Justice Charles the jury retired to return within thirty minutes with a verdict of guilty but insane. The sentence was that Sydney Pricket be kept as a criminal lunatic. Shortly afterwards the prisoner was conveyed to Broadmoor.

CHAPTER FIFTEEN

THE MANSLAUGHTER OF INSPECTOR FRANCIS JOHN EAST

Did he fall or was he pushed? That was the decision a court martial had to make in November 1944. Two American servicemen were charged with manslaughter and failing to give assistance.

On the evening of 4 October 1944, Sergeant Estle James Styles of Georgia and Private Frank Phillips of Carolina were chatting up two girls in Maidenhead. The scene was Castle Hill outside the county girls' school. Styles had cause to leave Phillips with the girls while he searched for a late-opening tobacconist. When he returned he found his friend indulging in a violent altercation with some local lads. Phillips was holding a monkey wrench to keep the locals at bay. Styles joined in the mêlée and a violent fracas ensued.

Police Inspector Francis John East was on duty in Maidenhead High Street when he was informed of the disturbance during his 8 p.m. call from a police box. East proceeded to Castle Hill where the physical affray had ended but verbal abuse and threats were coming in abundance from all sides.

Inspector East's presence quelled the situation a little. He proceeded to take the names and numbers of the two Americans. Having completed this he turned to take the names of the local civilians. Seeing this as an opportunity for escape Styles and Phillips jumped into an American Army weapon transporter and shot away from Castle Hill towards Reading.

Inspector East, deciding he had more questions to put to the servicemen, leaped on to the vehicle's running board in an attempt to detain them. The transporter travelled some 400 yards up the steep gradient before East was thrown off. He hit the ground with great force before his body was run over by a speeding saloon car. Inspector Francis John East, aged forty, died of his injuries several minutes later.

At the November court martial in front of Lieutenant-Colonel Leon

Castle Hill, Maidenhead, where in 1944 Police Inspector Francis John East fell, or was pushed to his death from an American Army weapon transporter. (Photograph by P. Bourne)

Ashjian, the prosecution was conducted by Captain Myron Byrawalt and the defence by Second Lieutenant Richard W. Dudley. Styles and Phillips entered a plea of not guilty. Dr John Mills, pathologist at Reading's Royal Berkshire, stated that East had died of multiple injuries, haemorrhage, shock and a fractured skull. He also mentioned that there was a bruise on the jaw that he found inconsistent with the other injuries.

Evidence was given of the brawl but this was brief, it was decided that the affray had only a partial bearing on the case against the two servicemen. William T. Westall of 96 Boyn Valley deposed that he was following a blue saloon car that was going at great speed when it went over the officer's body; the driver of the saloon did not stop.

A statement that Phillips had previously made to an American detective was then read to the court. The main points the young private made in his own defence were that he believed that East had finished with them once he had taken their details and that when Styles had told him to drive away he had not realized East was on the running board. Also he stated that after a couple of blocks, when he did realize the officer was on the running board, he assumed that East would jump off. As far as he was concerned, far from pushing the officer off, Styles was trying to prevent East from falling.

When Sergeant Styles took the stand he explained that he had assumed that East had sufficient information when he had ascertained their names, ranks and numbers. He had therefore told Phillips to drive away. East had proceeded to run after the truck, jumping on to the running board and grabbing him (Styles) by the forearms.

Styles had once again informed East that they had provided him with all the relevant information he needed but East persisted in hanging on. As the vehicle gained speed Styles had realized that the inspector was slipping and had desperately tried to hang on to him. Unfortunately East had fallen.

After a brief recess, a verdict of guilty as charged was brought in against the two young Americans. Phillips and Styles were both given dishonourable discharges and sentenced to three years' hard labour.

CHAPTER SIXTEEN

SLAUGHTER AT A VILLAGE INN – THREE MURDERED AT KINGSCLERE

There are many secrets of the Second World War. There were cover-ups on vast scales for varying reasons: some because had errors been disclosed they would have plainly illustrated the bungling inefficiences of men in whom nations had such unimpeachable faith; others because to relate the heinous nature of the events would disgust and mortify the general populace beyond human acceptance; and still others because if certain circumstances were to be released they would irretrievably damage the veneer of cordiality shared with our closest allies.

The horrific triple murder in a village on the Berkshire/Hampshire border was a classic candidate for a total blackout. It qualified on all accounts. It was brought about in part by inefficiency, it was abhorrent in the extreme and it was a total embarrassment to two Allied governments. Hence one of the most complete and impenetrable cover-ups of modern history.

The vast majority of American servicemen stationed in Britain during the war were fairly well liked, their popularity varying in degree according to which category of the local populace was judging it. Their overpoweringly confident and friendly company was highly favoured by local kids who enjoyed the never-ending supply of sweets and chewing gum. It was appreciated by the girls starved of nylon stockings and the sensual fulfilments of the flesh. It was tolerated by shopkeepers and publicans who were financially needy and was grudgingly ignored by what remained of the prime male population, the youths of the day contributing to the opinion that the yanks were 'overpaid, oversexed and over here'.

In fact the rapport created between inflicted host and enforced guest was in most cases warm and genuine; notwithstanding the occasional fist fight with the local lads, harmony reigned.

There are, however, bad apples in every barrel and the village of

Kingsclere near Newbury was experiencing more than its fair share of them. The servicemen stationed at Sydmonton Court were the most despised of all the US GIs, many of them illiterate and violent men.

By October 1944 the locals had had enough. Burglary, house-breaking and assault were daily occurrences. There had also been several rapes. Things had reached such a state that a specially commissioned police report had been sent to General Eisenhower personally.

On Thursday 5 October 1944, three or four American military policemen (MPs) were socializing with locals at the Crown Hotel in Kingsclere. The atmosphere was jovial and congenial.

At around 8 p.m. ten US servicemen entered the bar. Two of the MPs, Privates J.J. Anderson and J.W. Coates, straight away approached the men and requested to see their passes. The documents not being produced, the men were directed back to their quarters at Sydmonton Court under protest.

On returning to camp the men immediately withdrew loaded rifles and headed once more for Kingsclere, unbelievably without being challenged.

It was nearing closing time at 10 p.m. when gunfire was heard outside the small inn. Private Anderson went to the door to remonstrate. He was immediately cut down by several bullets. Private Coates was fatally wounded by bullets fired from several different directions through the public house window. He managed to jump out of another window and run 50 yards towards his assailants before he died in the tiny village square.

Fred Washington, a third MP, Mr Frederick Napper the landlord and several locals managed to hit the floor as bullets ricocheted around the room. At the same instant Mrs Rose Napper screamed, clutching her face where a bullet had passed through her cheek and immediately entered her brain, causing instant death.

By this time Washington was returning fire from a position of concealment. It was later found that one serviceman had been hit in the face and another in the hand.

After an age of screaming and disturbance, with ambulance bells blitzing the cold winter night, silence finally descended on the village.

The above is a less than perfect account of what occurred in the village of Kingsclere on 5 October 1944. It has been painstakingly gleaned from tacit and sometimes blatantly hostile sources. I can vouch for names and occupations of the people that died, but the sequence of events is open to

Hushed up during the Second World War: three people were slaughtered at The Crown at Kingsclere by American GIs. (Photograph by P. Bourne)

conjecture, there being little or no formative evidence. Even less precise and less communicative are the few contested facts that managed to seep through the brickwork of the wall of silence around the court martial. The men were charged with the murders of Mrs Rose Amelia Napper, Private J.J. Anderson and Private J.W. Coates. The case was heard at Thatcham.

The evidence that filtered through to the outside world was virtually non-existent, but we may take it that during the two-day hearing (8 and 9 November) much was heard.

One testimony that I did manage to trace was given by a Mr Henry James Walls, a ballistics expert from the Metropolitan police laboratories. Walls stated that he had traced thirty-three expended shell cases, fifteen of them from the carbine of Fred Washington, six from a rifle issued to a prisoner named Lawson. The others had all been individually fired from five separate riles. Walls was prepared to state that at least four of the remaining rifles had not been fired recently.

One indisputable fact that did emerge from the trial was that justice was done, if not seen to be done. Despite the black-out on all media a short statement was issued; it announced that nine of the men accused had been found guilty and sentenced to life imprisonment.

Since writing this rather threadbare narrative, with the new facts available, it has come to my notice that a Mr George Long (no relation), a local magistrate, wrote an exposé of the incident in 1961. I believe this was published in the *Hampshire Magazine,* but I have as yet been unable to obtain a copy.

CHAPTER SEVENTEEN

THE MURDER OF WILLIAM BISSETT BY GYPSY JOE SMITH, DECEMBER 1947

Mr William Bissett was a leading light in the small community of Wraysbury, a village lying between Slough and Staines. In December 1947 Bissett had reached the age of seventy-one. Tall at 6 feet 2 inches, and a robust 17 stone, he was enjoying retirement and indulging the majority of his leisure time in the three associations he had been affiliated to for years: the Freemasons, the Oddfellows and the Foresters.

It was after doing some charity business on Sunday 21 December that Bissett dropped into The Cock Inn at Staines. He indulged in polite conversation with three gypsy men standing at the bar. At closing time Bissett had been enticed by one of the three to accompany him home to Wraysbury to select a turkey. The destination was not far out of the way for Bissett who lived in Church Lane, probably about a mile off-course, which was nothing to this hardy old man who had a passion for walking.

William Bissett's disappearance was reported next day, Monday 22 December. Superintendent Gee of Slough CID was placed in charge, ably assisted by Superintendent Rawlings and Detective Inspector Pierson. A special inquiry was arranged for that evening and evidence concerning the three gypsies was heard. They were soon traced to Queens Mead, Wraysbury, an encampment by a small stream. Superintendent Gee detained them the same day; however, he released two the following morning, remanding only Joseph Smith, aged twenty-four, of The Halt, Wraysbury.

Smith was already making statements in plenty, mostly contradictory and suspect in the extreme. In the first statement he did not deny travelling home with Bissett but he swore that he had left him at a fork in the road, the old man heading for Church Street while Smith had returned home by way of crossing the stream.

A second statement by Smith taken that evening was somewhat changed from its predecessor. The story now was that Bissett had been drunk and stumbled across him. Smith, thinking he was being attacked, struck Bissett on the jaw and left him lying in the road.

Later, Smith made a third statement. In this account, he stated that after punching Bissett in the mouth, he had stolen his gold watch and chain and about £30 in notes, but this time Smith emphasized that after the attack he had watched the old man get up and walk away.

Smith told Superintendent Gee he had hidden the watch and chain near the gypsy camp. Later that day he accompanied the officer there and the items were retrieved. The following day a squad of officers under Detective Sergeant Harman thoroughly searched the surrounding area. Many items came to light; in a shed was found a pair of ex-RAF trousers, which were wet and bloodstained up to the knee. Smith admitted ownership and also that he had worn them on the night of Bissett's disappearance.

Shortly after, the police found a sack buried close to the stream; it contained Bissett's overcoat, jacket and trousers. In a matter of minutes William Bissett's body was discovered clad only in shirt and underpants which had been pulled down around his ankles. The body was found on its back in the stream but with the nose and mouth clear of the water. It was transported to Staines where the coroner Mr Nickson opened and closed an inquest within an hour. He adjourned proceedings awaiting laboratory and pathologists' reports.

This case was then to involve Dr Keith Simpson (later to become Professor Simpson), arguably Britain's most famous and accomplished pathologist. This case, however, was to give the illustrious doctor a few headaches. The trouble was the contradictory nature of scientific reports.

Simpson decided to send the contents of the stomach to Dr Holden at the Metropolitan Police laboratories. Along with these he sent some samples of grit and water from the stream. Holden discovered similar particles in the stomach. This was perplexing for Simpson as he had already discovered that Bissett had not drowned, and also by skin and water tests he had decided that the victim had been dead for two or three days, but the body had been in the water only some eighteen or twenty-four hours before its discovery.

Directly opposed to this was Holden's discovery of the particles. If, as

Simpson supposed, Bissett had been dead some two days before being immersed in the stream, how had he managed to draw the contents of that same stream into his stomach? The only way was by swallowing, and men who have been dead for several days do not swallow.

Police reports showed that the victim had received seven blows to the head and chest. One of these, to the left eye, had caused the head to jerk back and brought about a dislocation of the neck. There were also injuries to the brain membrane. Simpson stated that these injuries were severe enough to cause death after a short time. There were scratches on the legs and thighs suggesting that the body had been dragged by the shoulders or arms after death. Finally and significantly a couple of strands of Smith's hair were found clutched in the victim's fist.

Police were worried about many aspects of the case. They had found Bissett's blood group on Smith's trousers but why were the same trousers wet to the knee when the stream was barely ankle deep? For what reason had Bissett's outer clothing been removed and secreted at the gypsy camp? Where had the body been hidden between Bissett's demise and his baptism?

If, as the lab suggested, immersion had preceded death, a clever defence lawyer could argue that no murder had taken place. Merely robbery with violence, after which the unfortunate victim had stumbled into the stream swallowing water before expiring. Obviously though, this would not account for the underwear being around the body's ankles (an old gypsy trick to avoid pursuit), or for the scratches on the body that had been caused by it being dragged.

Simpson thought long on various scenarios before coming up with the right one. Bissett, gravely injured but not as yet dead, was transported across the stream by Smith and several colleagues to be concealed in the gypsy encampment, his dry outer clothing being carried separately. Midway, Bissett, a man of 17 stone, was almost certainly dropped by the inebriated men. At this time Bissett gulped water before being lifted again for the remainder of his unsteady final journey. This would also account for Smith's trousers being wet to the knees. After two days the body was dragged out and replaced beside the stream, sustaining its tell-tale drag scratches on its journey.

This was the sequence of events that the jury accepted as truth when

Dr Keith Simpson finally solved the contradictions presented by the body of
William Bissett

Lord Chief Justice Goddard turned down the appeal of gypsy Joe Smith

Joseph Smith came up for trial at Kingston Assizes on 3 March 1948.

Smith was represented by Mr W.L. Raeburn KC and Mr W.T. Wells. Against insurmountable evidence Smith reverted to his story of leaving Bissett alive after robbing him. Taking Simpson's estimation of the time of death, he invented an alibi which would have placed him well out of the area at the agreed time. He insisted that he was visiting a gypsy named Belcher Lee in his tent at Iver in Buckinghamshire. Mr Raeburn laboured the point most eloquently but he must have realized he was clutching at straws.

Another avenue for the defence thoroughly exploited by Mr Raeburn was the fact that, if the 17 stone body of Bissett had been carried over the stream and to the encampment and back, someone must have helped Smith to do it. There were no able-bodied men other than Smith at the camp during those few days.

The prosecution denied this point and suggested that the two men who had initially been questioned with Smith (his uncle and his father-in-law), although advanced in years, were still robust and hardy.

Mr Justice Oliver was brief in his summing-up. He told the jury to ask themselves one question. If Smith hadn't killed Mr Bissett who on earth could have done? If he had merely struck him and robbed him, why hadn't Bissett gone home? Nobody else surely would have any reason for harming him or robbing him. He had nothing left, not even his clothing.

The jury retired for twenty minutes before returning with a verdict of guilty. Mr Justice Oliver's voice quavered as he pronounced the death sentence. Smith's pregnant young wife collapsed as she heard it and some thirty or more hostile gypsies stormed from the room.

An appeal was heard on Tuesday 6 April with Mr Raeburn KC suggesting that the jury had been misdirected on certain points at the original trial. Lord Chief Justice Goddard was having none of it. 'It was a clear-cut case of murder,' he announced as he turned down the appeal.

CHAPTER EIGHTEEN

THE MAIDENHEAD TRUNK MURDER OF MINNIE FREEMAN-LEE

In the preface to this book I mention that a couple of these stories had been published before. This is one of them. It is included solely because it is local and necessary for a full record of Berkshire murders.

In the latter years of the nineteenth century Mrs Minnie Freeman-Lee had been a celebrated beauty and socialite; attractive, intelligent and sparkling in conversation, she had adorned the company of parties and receptions in Monte Carlo, Paris, Vienna, London and Rome. By the early part of the new century Minnie, by then married to a barrister and with a handsome young son, was settled in England.

In 1908 the family was living in Maidenhead in a seventeen-roomed red brick rambling house. The house, named Wynford, was situated in the town's exclusive Ray Park Avenue, which was still festooned with beautiful socialites and accomplished persons of every profession.

Unfortunately Minnie was deprived of her son by the Great War, which was a tragic loss to doting parents. Minnie's husband followed in the 1930s, leaving her alone in the vast but desirable property.

Over the years the property and owner became less desirable; the house and its occupier were slipping into disrepair. By 1948 Minnie, then aged eighty-eight (some reports even state ninety-four), had elected to live in one room only. Fine furniture now sadly suffering from neglect had been stacked all over the house as Minnie had retreated to a front-room lounge.

Minnie, however, could not be enticed from her dilapidated mansion of memories into any council-run hostelry. She stubbornly refused to leave. This of course helped endorse the speculative rumours that Minnie was 'sitting on a goldmine', a story inevitably put around about any aged eccentric.

It was later to be proved that she was definitely not guarding a hoard of money. Minnie was living on £6 a week from a benevolent society and

The Thames Hotel, Maidenhead, where recluse Minnie Freeman-Lee occasionally dined. A rare and appreciated treat. (Photograph by P. Bourne)

received her daily sustenance from the 'Meals on Wheels'. Her luxuries were forty cigarettes a day, which she collected herself, and the occasional lunch at the Thames Hotel.

On 1 June 1948 milkman George Rome was delivering in Ray Park Avenue. At Wynford he noticed that the previous day's delivery had not been taken into the house. Thinking this a little odd he broached the subject with a close neighbour, Mr Arthur Hilsdon. Deciding that the situation needed further investigation the two men returned to Wynford and knocked and called out. On receiving no reply they pushed open the door that was permanently unlocked, and entered.

The place was in a terrible shambles, which they both knew to be its permanent condition, but somehow the mess was more systematic than usual, as if somebody had ransacked the muddle with a purpose in mind. The men looked in every room and called Minnie's name but the search remained fruitless. Fruitless, that is, except for a couple of items that

The gruesome remains of Minnie Freeman-Lee, discovered by solicitor Mr Ruffe-Thomas when he inadvertently opened the trunk

caused some concern. They had found Minnie's bunch of keys on the landing and close by a black court shoe, one of a pair that the eccentric old lady wore constantly.

George Rome and Arthur Hilsdon decided that this was a police matter. They contacted the police and were quickly joined by PC George Langton. The constable in turn initiated his own search of the premises which turned out to be as unsuccessful as the previous two.

Finally Mrs Freeman-Lee's solicitor was contacted, a young man named Kenneth Ruffe-Thomas, who lived nearby in the same exclusive street of Ray Park Avenue.

Mr Ruffe-Thomas had been called in by PC Langton purely in an advisory capacity. Langton knew that if Mrs Freeman-Lee had planned on going away she would certainly have left word with her solicitor. Ruffe-Thomas, however, could throw no light upon her whereabouts, but while the four men were in conversation the young solicitor was absentmindedly playing with the fastenings of a trunk, an ancient affair resting on the domestic debris. All of a sudden the lid sprang open revealing its contents to an alarmed quartet. The gagged and bound corpse of the eccentric widow was revealed.

Superintendent W.J. Crombie of Reading CID was immediately brought in on the case. He was ably assisted by Superintendent W.H. Benstead of Maidenhead. Crombie was able to ascertain through diligent enquiries that the last person to see Mrs Freeman-Lee alive was an electrician who had done a repair and had left at 6.20 p.m. on Saturday 29 May.

The time of death could be estimated at being at any point between the evening of 29 May and the discovery of the body on the morning of 1 June. Dr Keith Simpson, already so described, could be only a little more specific. When he arrived with his inseparable assistant Miss Scott-Dunn on the afternoon of 2 June he deduced that life had been extinguished some forty-eight hours previously. Simpson examined bruises on Minnie's head and decided that they were not of a severity to kill her; this contradicted what various newspapers had stated, namely that Mrs Freeman-Lee had been bludgeoned to death.

Death had been brought about by asphyxia, Dr Simpson assured the police. The victim had been crammed into the trunk alive and then left to suffocate. A more detailed description of the sequence of events would be that Mrs Freeman-Lee had been attacked and struck several times around the head, her hands had been tied behind her back with a shawl and she had also been gagged. The gag had become congested with mucus and saliva, this had obstructed the pores in the cloth, the victim had then struggled causing her breathing to become more laboured; this action only worsened matters and caused a fatal vicious circle.

On 3 June the big guns of Scotland Yard were brought in on the case. Superintendent W. Chapman of the Flying Squad arrived, accompanied by Detective Sergeant Hislop. The erubescent Chapman, known affectionately as 'Cherub', had disentangled what had seemed to be the unsolvable Luton Sack Case some five years previously.

Soon after 'Cherub' there arrived Chief Superintendent Frederick Cherrill, the Yard's greatest fingerprint expert.

Cherrill set to work in his own meticulously methodical way, but after many hours his efforts remained unrewarded. He knew he was dealing with

Chief Superintendent Frederick Cherrill, the world's leading fingerprint expert, whose meticulous tenacity brought about the conviction of George Russell

a professional, a man who would certainly have worn gloves. The chief superintendent's hopes were fading; he knew that if this man was going to be caught, the best hope would be through fingerprints, and there weren't any.

While searching through the entanglement of bedding Cherrill came across a 2 inch square, lidless jewellery box; he tested it for fingerprints but found nothing. He searched for the lid and after some difficulty discovered it under the bed. It had been squashed flat where it had been trodden on. Cherrill dusted the lid and found two faint fragments of fingerprints, each less than 5/16 of an inch in length. It was next to nothing but it might just suffice. He rushed the lid to his colleague Chief Inspector Holten at the Yard. Holten matched the prints in record time; they belonged to a man who had been on the Yard's books since 1933 when he was arrested at Oxford, an itinerant Irish labourer named George Russell.

Within a week, 45-year-old George Russell was in custody. He was arrested at St Albans at a hostel. In his possession was a silk scarf that was identified as belonging to Minnie Freeman-Lee. Russell swore that he had purchased it for a shilling off a man at an hostel in London. On returning to Maidenhead it was discovered that Russell was known to the local police, he had been working as a jobbing gardener in the area and had been pulled in for several misdemeanours. He had also worked at a Maidenhead hotel.

Superintendent Chapman escorted Russell to Wynford in Ray Park Avenue for questioning. This is an old trick that has achieved varying results over the years, the theory being that once confronted by the scene of the crime the accused is more likely to break down completely or, at the very least, inadvertently give himself away.

It was partially effective with Russell. When questioned about his fingerprints and the scarf he broke down in tears, but he would admit to nothing other than calling at the house once with an offer to do some gardening. Russell was remanded to Oxford prison to await the assizes at Reading in October.

At the assizes George Russell appeared before Mr Justice Hallett, an elderly gentleman renowned for his many and often pointless interruptions

Boulters Lock, a much frequented beauty spot, just a stone's throw away from the decaying body of Minnie Freeman-Lee

of barristers' speeches. Hallett was, however, a very astute and adroit lawyer himself.

Incidentally Keith Simpson was later to observe that he found it ironic, especially for this particular case, that the venerable Hallett had on his desk a couple of volumes of law entitled *Russell on Crime*.

George Russell virtually convicted himself from the box when he made the statement: 'Did I murder this poor aged woman for something she was supposed to have, but had not? No, I did not figure in such a murder.' To everybody in the room this was tantamount to a confession. How could Russell know poor Minnie had nothing unless he had searched the room expecting to find something?

In summing up Mr Justice Hallett informed the jury that if an intruder were to use violence on his victim whilst executing that intrusion, and that violence resulted in the victim's death, then as a point of law this violence that resulted in death should be adjuged as murder.

He continued, 'Either Russell or the police were telling lies. Was Russell extremely unlucky? Had he been at the hostel at the wrong time and bought the scarf at the wrong time from the wrong man?'

Justice Hallett showed by his countenance that he found this scenario absurd. He went on to the police evidence and in particular that of Chief Superintendent Frederick Cherrill: 'This officer has no doubt that these were Russell's fingerprints.' He inferred who else's if not those of the murderer. The jury was out for two hours, longer than expected. They returned with a verdict of guilty as charged. Mr Justice Hallett had no hesitation in sentencing Russell to death. An appeal was turned down in mid-November and George Russell was hanged at Oxford prison on 2 December 1948.